Contemporary International Glass 60 Artists in the V&A

Glass

Contemporary International

60 Artists in the V&A

Jennifer Hawkins Opie

V&A Publications

First published by V&A Publications, 2004
V&A Publications
160 Brompton Road
London SW3 1HW

Distributed in North America by Harry N. Abrams,
Incorporated, New York

Jennifer Hawkins Opie asserts her moral right to be
identified as the author of this book

ISBN 1 85177 4262

Library of Congress Control Number 2004103249

A catalogue record for this book is available from the
British Library.

Designed by Broadbase
New V&A photography by Sara Hodges,
V&A Photographic Studio

Front jacket illustration: Colin Reid, Untitled. See p.108
Back jacket illustration: Mieke Groot, Untitled. See p.54
Frontispiece: Angela Jarman, Evolution 1. See p.66

Printed in China

V&A Publications
160 Brompton Road
London SW3 1HW
www.vam.ac.uk

Contents

The Collection

Glass is a responsive, challenging and vivid material for artists. It is also a practical, waterproof, unobtrusive material for design in daily use. It is special and everyday, flamboyant and functional, collected and discarded. The V&A Museum's collection contains both types – both special and everyday – but this book celebrates exclusively the use of glass by artists.

The Museum has acquired glass by artists since the 1960s. The selection has been driven by a variety of circumstances, opportunities and rationales and the growth of the collection has not been consistent. Around 1990, however, it began to take on a shape and significance worthy of the V&A. It has grown to include works from abroad by internationally celebrated artists from as far afield as America and Australia, with others from continental Europe. While the Museum's ambitions still run high for the inclusion of an even wider spread of key makers, the V&A collection, as it stands now, is already unrivalled in the UK. This book celebrates the collection, and sets down markers for its future growth.

Despite the increasing volume of critical literature on glass art, and its general popularity, there remains a degree of confusion about its identity. If the essay that follows appears insistent it is for this very reason. Art Glass, Studio Glass and Glass Art are each terms that have a precise history. But they are all frequently used in ways that misrepresent the practice of making non-utility objects in glass. This practice is conducted by artists who choose to employ glass, and the work is called Glass Art.

From Studio Glass to Glass Art

'Studio Glass' is widely understood to refer to unique work handmade by a single artist-maker. It is distinct from factory-made decorative wares in which the artist has no direct or practical input, which is professionally designed and passed to employed glass-making teams for multiple production. The way of working by one single, driven individual and the unique product, 'studio glass', were finally defined and named in the 1960s. The definition took root so firmly that, even now, it is still commonly held as a benchmark for the genuine article. Even now, the most commonly asked question is 'Does he make it himself?' If the answer is 'No', or, 'Only in part', interest begins to wane and the glasswork is perceived to be of lesser status. However, this categorization no longer holds good as will be explained in the following pages.

Before 'studio glass' there was 'art glass', the term used for the work of Emile Gallé, Louis Comfort Tiffany and their contemporaries in the 1890s, the period of Art Nouveau. 'Art Glass' was designed by artists like Gallé and Tiffany who were also factory-owners. It was realized by them in close collaboration with their employees, the skilled craftsmen. At their best and least commercial, 'art glass' productions were unique, or made in limited numbers, and all with a high degree of hand-finishing (PLATE 1).

The recent history of 'studio glass' has been thoroughly covered in many publications so here it need only be summarized.[1]

1 BELOW
Emile Gallé
Vase du Chêne
France, about 1895
V&A: C.599-1920

2 OPPOSITE, TOP
Maurice Marinot
France, 1932
V&A: C.13-1964

3 OPPOSITE, BELOW
Harvey Littleton
USA, 1965
V&A: Circ.240-1967

'Studio Glass' is a comparatively recently coined term, but even during Gallé's time there were individual artists working to acquire the skills of glassmaking for themselves. France remained the centre. In the 1880s, Henry Cros laboriously invented *pâte de verre* by himself, unaware of the factory-owner, Georges Despret, who achieved virtually the same process in Belgium at about the same time. Cros's secret recipes were taken up by his son, Jean. Albert Dammouse and, after him, François Décorchemont, followed with variations on the same technique. During the 1920s and 1930s Maurice Marinot designed and made his own glass in a separated area within a factory. Exhibiting with the Fauve group of painters, Marinot learned the glass techniques for himself and is now generally recognized as the first major artist in glass (PLATE 2). Less well known, during the 1940s the independent Jean Sala ran his own studio in Paris.

Outside France and rather more commercial than either Marinot or Sala, the Ysart family team was responsible for the conception and realization of their own glass at their studio workshop in Perth, Scotland, from 1946. During the 1950s, the key example of a single name associated with studio glass is that of Erwin Eisch. The Eisch family owned their own glass business, in Frauenau, and still do. Erwin Eisch took advantage of this to experiment with sculptural glass. His most celebrated form is the portrait head, in which he has specialized throughout his long career (PAGE 40).

In the 1950s in America, several artist-makers, working independently, had begun to establish a network of like-minded artists, the hallmark of any new art movement. They were all exclusively engaged in kiln-forming – the relatively painstaking, time-consuming processes of fusing, slumping, enamelling and lampworking. The breakthrough came with the possibility of blowing molten glass, with its immediacy and inherent drama, outside a factory setting.

The development during the very early 1960s of the small pot kiln (for the containment of molten glass) – which can be set up anywhere and is manageable by one artist-maker – and the timely availability of a glass type which melts at low temperatures and is suitable for blowing, combined to give this emerging generation the means to express itself in glass. The only restraint was the artists' imagination, and their lack of experience in managing free-flowing hot glass – recognizing the need for which, and acquiring the techniques, came later. These technical developments were achieved in the United States through the energies of Harvey Littleton, a ceramist and son of the director of research at Corning Glass Works (PLATE 3).

Although Littleton was well aware of Eisch and Sala, having visited Europe during the 1950s, there were reasons why the distinctly American advances have taken precedence in the history of studio glass. The fact that these were so widely trumpeted and, more particularly, that they were followed by teaching courses promulgating the Littleton message, is especially significant. Equally, the fact that the first graduates from these courses also travelled with a missionary zeal, taking the message of hot glass (for it was blown glass by which these pioneers were most enthralled) abroad, also serves to give the American history mythic proportions.

In the UK, Sam Herman was the most important of these graduates, arriving in 1965. He built the first of these new kilns at Edinburgh, then at the Royal College of Art in London, and converted students there to this new and exciting glass activity (PLATE 4). Ten years later he did the same in Australia. By the later 1960s and throughout the 1970s international conferences, competitions and exhibitions held in the United States, Europe, Japan and Australia all helped to spread the message.

Since the 1980s the concept of studio glass has changed its shape again. Curiously, although most people understand the word 'studio' to mean a place where an individual artist works to produce art, the leap from 'studio glass' to 'glass art' still raises eyebrows. This is where the difficult and apparently contentious word 'craft' enters the picture. Glass-makers who aspire to the 'superior' designation of 'artist' find that designation questioned. It seems it is the actual material that requires justification. Undoubtedly functionality is an issue. Glass is firmly identified with utility – drinking from, or looking through; utility requires craft to make it work. Collectively, the crafts are still regarded as a poor relation to art even now, despite decades passing since the first breaching of the barriers by visionary artists like Stanislav Libenský and Jaroslava Brychtová in the 1960s (PLATE 5) and others who followed, like Clifford Rainey in the 1980s.

Art and Craft

As so many artist-makers are placed on one side or the other of the divide between art and craft by their audience – collectors and critics – it is worth attempting to set the record straight and to give each its due.

'Craft' is an interesting word with a long history. At times since the 15th century, when it first appears, it has meant 'occult art, magic, strength, power, force, device, artifice, expedient, a branch of learning' and a 'science'. Today it means 'skill, art, occupation'. Literally, 'crafty' means 'artful'. 'Handicraft' is a 'manual art'. A craftsman is one who practises a handicraft, an artist 'one who cultivates one of the fine arts'.[2] In other words, craft and its derivatives are complex terms which originally were attractive and elevating. The successful laying on of paint on a prepared ground, the skill required to cast a bronze form from an original model in wax or plaster, or to chisel a form from a marble block are all hard-won crafts requiring years of practice. The term 'craftsman' is an honourable one. Craft is admirable, satisfying. A basket woven with a consummate skill and deep understanding of form and function handed down through generations, a staircase exquisitely proportioned and constructed after a lengthy apprenticeship will each be a source of immense satisfaction, of visual and tactile pleasure. A perfectly blown or expertly cast and proportioned vase or goblet will be equally so. Recently the craftsman has

been defined as one 'who strove to create a perfectly executed functional object from the finest glass possible'.[3]

Although the hierarchy had been debated in the 16th century in Italy, the term, fine art, is a much younger one, deriving from the late 18th-century French *beaux-arts* – the arts which 'are concerned with the beautiful or which appeal to taste'.[4] These 'beautiful arts' are understood to be Painting, Sculpture and, less commonly now, Architecture. The superiority of France as arbiter of taste (and expense) was fully established by the 19th century and still holds good. If in doubt of their taste or if in need to impress with symbols universally understood, palaces and smart hotels from America through Europe to the Orient are furnished in French 18th-century style. Fine art therefore has an unarguable pedigree with a track record of superior patronage.

There is a third term, less clearly defined but of crystal clarity in the minds of those who use it, which is 'decorative'. It is often perceived as a perjorative term. Glass, and indeed all the materials normally associated with crafts, can be swept into this catch-all repository. Thus the hierarchy is reinforced.

In 1899 the Art Nouveau designer Henry van de Velde, like several of his contemporaries, was concerned about the artificial barriers put up between the fine arts and the others. The emerging concept of 'art for living' and the 'complete work of art' – a building with the full internal panoply of paintings, furniture, textiles, ceramics, and glass – depends on an acceptance of equality in all the arts.[5] Van de Velde said, 'It is important to note that all terminology, like low art, art of second rank, art industry, decorative art and arts and crafts is only valid as long as one agrees with it. However, this does not imply that these terms are just or that the situation they describe really means anything.'[6] Two years earlier, in 1897, Gallé said, 'Let us not tire of saying over and over again that there are no castes among the artisans of art, that there are no mean and plebeian arts.'[7]

In 1962, the Norwegian glass historian, Ada Polak, wrote, 'Our period has also been the age of the glass artist. (In English the expression is strange and awkward, whereas the French *artiste verrier* and the German *Glaskünstler* have long been accepted.) We have seen how he emerged in France during the latter part of the nineteenth century, and how the ambition to make glassmaking an art, on a par with painting and sculpture, has inspired producers of glass in many countries to their finest achievements.'

In the same year, the Czech glass professor in whose studio many of the greatest artists trained, Josef Kaplický, said, 'There is only one Art. There is no Great Art on the one hand and some decorative, coquettish, applied art on the other hand. It is not possible that applied art should lag behind "pure art" in the depth of its conceptions. It too must be the most serious record of the heartbeat of the time. Otherwise it would be only a mockery unworthy of life-long endeavour, unworthy of a grown-up man.'[9]

In 1968 in London Harvey Littleton attempted to put to rest these divisions, yet attitudes to art and craft continued to be polarized throughout the 1970s and 1980s.[10] Most recently, the British maker and theorist, Keith Cummings – author of seminal books on the techniques of kiln-formed glass and teacher of a generation of present-day makers – has written succinctly and expressively about the many and complex factors in the making processes and the use of glass as an 'expressive medium'.[11]

Today, the distinctions are blurred. Even now, few miss the opportunity to have their work linked with 'fine art', yet most artists, makers and much of their well-informed audience would admit, like Gallé, that the distinction is irrelevant. Now, artists may come from other disciplines and choose to use glass along with metal, wood or stone – each with its own particular characteristic. Glass craftsmen and women want to stretch the material to its limits to make objects – sculptures – with that extra breath of thoughtfulness, that straining towards intellectual ambition, which claims the title of 'art'. Now artists come from both sides of the divide: those who are primarily sculptors whose choice of material, including glass, is driven by concept, and those whose mastery is in specialist glass-making techniques who want to use their skill to make sculptural objects.

Glass Art

Any art that engages with its audience in a thought-provoking way depends on some tension between the physical appeal of the materials, the skill in its production, and the intellectual ambitions of the artist.

Glass-making techniques of all sorts can take years to perfect. As a result, the preoccupation with technique – the 'how it is made' – can be so insistent that this is often thought sufficient justification for the glass artwork in its own right. On the other hand, of all materials glass is the most seductive. Even with minimal manipulation, it has qualities so universally appealing that any intellectual justification for using it is often thought unnecessary. Many glass-makers talk of light, translucency, brilliance, opacity, limpidity, depth and mystery as motivation enough for a lifetime's work and, indeed, meeting a common need for beauty and physical response is one of the artist's great contributions to the human experience.

In 1988 the glass artist, Max Jacquard, wrote about Clifford Rainey that he:

> has a problem with glass. He clearly loves its mysticism, its presence, but often it is so seductive, that it takes away the idea that it is portraying. When the piece goes in a gallery they're not meant to be looked at as 'Hey, this is really attractive,' I want people to look at them and think, 'What's this guy trying to get across?' He hopes eventually to reach the point where you could look at a piece and be unaware that it was made of glass because the overpowering thing would be what it portrays.[12] (PLATE 6)

For many artists the characteristics of glass, and the techniques required to control the material, are not enough. For them concept comes first, to

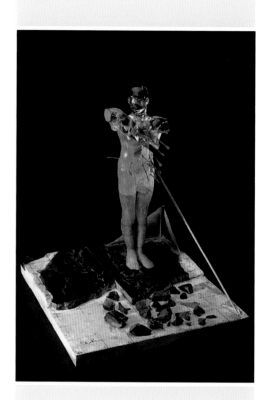

6 ABOVE
Clifford Rainey
Belfast after Pollaiuolo
UK, about 1981
V&A: C.70-1982

7 OPPOSITE
René Roubíček
Kohlrabi
Czechoslovakia, 1959
V&A: C.21-1998

the extent that if the technique is wanting, rather than spend more years in training they will collaborate with others who have mastered the required skills. As glass used in combination with other materials becomes commonplace, collaboration with a multi-skilled team has become increasingly the norm. It is this overriding need which has taken contemporary artists working in glass beyond the old confines of the 'studio glass' definition. In reality that definition barely survived the 1960s. By the early 1970s the value of teamwork and the advantages of sharing skills were already being taken up again. Not for nothing did several of today's artists as students experience the Venetian method of working as part of a team of skilled glass-blowers assembled under one master blower. The camaraderie between hot glass artists especially is one of the most attractive characteristics of their community. Artists who are international names will willingly lend their mastery of a particular technique to a fellow artist, playing a collaborative role, sometimes even a subservient one.

The Italian, Lino Tagliapietra – Muranese and a *maestro* by 1956 at the age of 22 – has always blown glass with masterly precision and Venetian flair. His consummate skill has been an acknowledged inspiration since his first visit to the United States in 1979. Since then, he and the Americans Dante Marioni and Richard Marquis, have been part of a close-knit, collaborative community. Others, like Neil Wilkin and Carl Nordbruch in the UK, with less of an international reputation in their own right, regularly hire out their skills and are highly respected and sought after for this service.

In the late 1950s, the Czech René Roubíček, manipulated free-flowing, hot glass in a series of untitled sculptures which appear to have a life rampantly independent of any maker. Of course, in reality he blew and worked the molten glass with knowledge and panache (PLATE 7). In a more experimental mode, in 1971 Dale Chihuly and James Carpenter allowed glass to fall as long ribbons, simply to see how far the glass would stretch. Both were still comparative novices, driven by curiosity rather than hard-won skill. The resulting glass forms were entirely due to the effects of heat, gravity and ductility – easy enough, although no one else was doing it. Chihuly always acknowledges a debt to the painter Jackson Pollock; another forerunner to these glass pioneers was the American Abstract Expressionist ceramicist, Peter Voulkos who, in the 1950s had attacked and subverted established principles for the working of clay on a massive scale. In the early 1970s, Post-minimalism was the movement of the moment and a climate of revolution and experiment in the 'lesser arts' was hardly new. But Chihuly and Carpenter grouped the glass ribbons together with similarly ribbon-like neon and argon strips, in a temporary installation which became a room-sized sculpture encouraging the physical engagement of the audience. In doing this, they took the work onto another plane and opened up the possibilities of glass as a material for large-scale, environmental sculpture.

Although the manipulation of hot glass has attracted so much attention

– because of its immediacy, the noise, heat and pace of its making and the enthusiasm of the pioneers of the 1960s – cast glass was established as a sculptural medium rather earlier, and with far less fanfare.

During the 1950s in Czechoslovakia, making sculptures on a monumental scale was not only possible but was encouraged as part of the communist state's programme of international promotion. This way of working emerged fully onto the world stage only in the Milan Triennale in 1957 and then the World's Fair in Brussels in 1958. There, architectural sculptures in melted, cast glass were a revelation to everyone who witnessed them. The most advanced of these sculptures were by the multi-skilled Roubíček, who used blown and cast elements in a large-scale installation, and by the emerging partnership of Stanislav Libenský and Jaroslava Brychtová.

With the invention that they called 'mould-melted' glass, this famous husband-and-wife team made possible the casting of sculptures on a hitherto unprecedented scale and of unimagined subtlety. Because they had no choice but to work in factory glassworks, Czech artists were able to use industrial quantities of glass and take advantage of the large-scale equipment to hand and the development of glass art in Czechoslovakia took a very different course from elsewhere. In addition to the technical differences, the Czech artists' isolation forced them to seek parallels and inspiration from entirely different sources. Cut off from intellectual exchange with their European and American contemporaries, they drew instead on the major movements of 20th-century painting – from Cubism in all its forms to Abstract Expressionism.

Thus, almost innocently, the Czechs proposed glass as an appropriate material for exploring sculptural abstraction. In this they opened up a world of possibilities. Whereas, some 30 years earlier, Marinot had made 'sculptural' glass which had virtually nothing to do with practical functionality, his vocabulary was, nevertheless, based on vase and bottle forms. Today, while many artists still choose to use the vessel form it is often as a metaphor in which containment or presentation are central.[13]

Technical variety grows with each decade. Most recently, the use of newer types of glass requires a fresh eye and an understanding of unfamiliar qualities. Borosilicate glass – its heat- and shock-resistant qualities developed for use in laboratories and the domestic kitchen – has been used by Richard Meitner (PAGE 84) and Danny Lane (PAGE 16).

Hardly new, painting on glass still attracts puzzlement or criticism on occasions, although it has a history older than painting on canvas. In the 15th and 16th centuries, painted and stained windows were made at a time when picture-painting was still done, as it had been for millennia, either directly on gessoed walls or wooden panels. Enamel-painted vessel-glass first appeared in Roman antiquity and was widely used by the 12th century AD in Egypt and Syria. It was common in central Europe and Italy by the 16th century and was continued in northern Europe, Bohemia especially, throughout the 19th century. In the earlier 1950s, Czech

8 OPPOSITE, TOP
Stanislav Libenský
1001 Nights
Czechoslovakia, 1946
V&A: C.104-1984

9 OPPOSITE, BELOW
Karel Vanura
Bottle
Czechoslovakia, 1959
V&A: C.103-1984

10 BELOW
Kyōhei Fujita
Red and White Plum Blossoms
Japan, 1988
V&A: FE.6&A-1989

artists maintained this tradition but their painting on glass was heavily influenced by contemporary 'fine art'. Stanislav Libenský and Karel Vanura, in different ways, demonstrated the vibrant possibilities of this ancient technique (PLATES 8, 9). Since then Dana Zámečníková (PAGE 136) and Bohumil Eliáš (PAGE 42) have used the technique as freely and expressively on glass as they might on canvas or paper.

The most celebrated of Japanese glass artists, Fujita Kyōhei, held his first exhibition in 1957, and in the late 1970s and early 1980s he spent time in Murano, and at Orrefors glassworks in Sweden. Fujita's most iconic series is of glass forms based on the traditional lidded, lacquerwork box. In this series he adopted not just the classic shape but, more surprisingly, the appearance of the ancient Japanese technique, by drawing on the equally ancient Italian mastery of the use of gold and spattered colours. The series is a contemporary Japanese statement in a highly personal glass language (PLATE 10).

Engraved glass is a particular speciality of northern Europe. The term can be widely interpreted to include almost any form of cutting into glass but the historic techniques of wheel-cutting and diamond-point engraving are the most commonly accepted. By the 17th century, with the development of a clear, hard glass suitable for engraving, the technique was especially the preserve of the German states, Bohemia and The Netherlands. Technical expertise spread further across Northern Europe and Britain during the 18th and 19th centuries. The 18th-century Dutch technique of stipple-engraving, building up a picture by means of minute dots, was revived, in a spirit of modernity by the British artist, Laurence Whistler, in the 1930s. Since then a dedicated school of British engravers working in this laborious method has sprung up.

In the 1950s the Australian John Hutton, used 'flexible drive' engraving for some of the most expressionist of images in the new Coventry Cathedral (PLATE 11).[14] In the 1960s, the master Czech engraver, Jiří Harcuba, used wheel-engraving in an equally expressive, painterly manner (PLATE 12). Today, Alison Kinnaird is one of Britain's most respected engravers (PAGE 70). Like painting, this diverse technique lends itself especially well to storytelling and the mixing and over-laying of images.

It is true that for some practitioners the nuances of nomenclature seem irrelevant, but for most, their rising ambition was fuelled by the proliferation (for a while at least) of glass courses in art schools where they were run alongside fine art departments. This gave birth to the new definition, that of Glass Art. Indeed, many glass artists are happy to drop the qualifier 'glass' from the title altogether. Undeniably, the challenge of selling has had much to do with this. Breaking into the world of fine art galleries boosts status and price. Galleries that specialize in glass – for example, Habatat, Heller, Traver and Foster-White, in the USA, and von Barthe in Switzerland – have their own distinctive exclusivity. But when the Piccadilly Gallery showed Clifford Rainey's sculptures in 1988, and the

Marlborough Gallery (best known for its sales of paintings and sculpture) accepted Chihuly's glass art in 2000, each occasion was considered a major breakthrough.

Breaking down other barriers, many artists working in glass have exhibited in venues not obviously suited to either glass or the crafts as part of the drive to increase audiences' accessibility to the art, and to provide further opportunities for artists. In London alone, the sculptor Emma Woffenden, has shown her work at The Wellcome Institute and the group, New London Glass held its opening show on Gloucester Road Underground station, followed by, in 2003, a highly successful exhibition in a variety of spaces in the Great Eastern Hotel. The dissolving of barriers is not one-way either. The British sculptors Richard Deacon and Tony Cragg have both used glass in major works shown at Tate Modern in London. Alison Wilding first used glass in 2001 at the North Lands school in northern Scotland. In 2003 the painter Chris Ofili used glass for the ceiling called *Afro Kaleidoscope*, part of his installation in the British Pavilion at the Venice Biennale.

The test of art in any material, glass included, is in its comparison with its contemporaries. Per B Sundberg's highly plastic *Guts* and Koichiro Yamamoto's statement on negative spaces in *Jug* and *Mug* (PAGE 134) both recall aspects of Surrealism; Erwin Eisch's *Head* (PAGE 40), Richard Meitner's *Alice* (PAGE 84) and Max Jacquard's *Brick Man* (PAGE 64) all lay claim to sculptural territory. Peter Aldridge's *A Moment in Time*, (PAGE 18) offers a sculptural and an architectural experience. Placing glass in an environment that itself becomes part of the work is a direction which many glass artists have taken and which makes the subsequent showing of the work a constant challenge (and the recording of the original setting vital). In some cases now the glass is ephemeral, it is the recording which is the work of art. Site-specific commissions and the designation 'landscape art' are common.

Conclusion

The glass world now is changing rapidly. Glass courses contract and expand. There is still no course in France. The department at the Gerrit Rietveld Academy in Amsterdam no longer has the exclusivity it had accrued. On the other hand, the exchange of ideas and practical information at international conferences is evidence of real growth. The Glass Art Society of America holds annual conferences of 2000 attendees. Smaller conferences, as well as competitions and international exhibitions, are held and arranged globally from Scotland to Japan. Journals and magazines add to the opportunities for communication and dissemination of ideas.

In the last two decades, glass has come of age as a material for a global art form. There is an increasing conviction that it is the material for the future – for art, and for science. Practitioners who would have been described as 'studio glass-makers' thirty years ago are now clearly in a different world. Now they have a right to claim some part of 'fine art'

11 BELOW
John Hutton
UK, 1958–9
V&A: C.28-1975

12 OPPOSITE
Jiří Harcuba
Czechoslovakia, 1965
V&A: Circ.188&A-1966

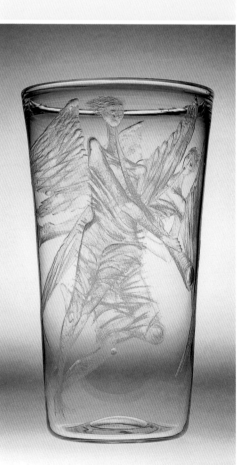

territory, and their art must be judged by the conception as well as the quality and skill in its making. Where they exploit the tension between the material and the technique they have chosen to employ, where they transcend the inherently easy seductiveness of glass to imprint something of themselves upon it, where they make a work of art with intellectual ambition, then they must be judged as artists. To attempt to define art, let alone 'good art' here would be to venture onto notoriously dangerous ground, certainly subjective and possibly futile. But if we accept for now Josef Kaplický's wise and thoughtful definition of art as 'the most serious record of the heartbeat of the time', that should be sufficient test.[15]

1   For example, Frantz, Susanne K, *Contemporary Glass*, Corning Museum of Glass, 1989; Klein, Dan, *Glass, a Contemporary Art*, William Collins & Co, 1989

2   *Shorter Oxford Dictionary*

3   Frantz, *Contemporary Glass*, as above, p.53

4   *Shorter Oxford Dictionary*

5   For full argument see Greenhalgh, Paul, 'The Style and the Age', *Art Nouveau 1890–1914*, V&A, 2003, pp.15–33

6   Van de Velde, Henry, *Allgeine bemerkungen zu einer synthese der Kunst*, Pan, August, 1899, pp.261–70, quoted in *Art Nouveau*, as above, p.20

7   Gallé, Emile, Sept. 1897, pp.229–50, quoted in *Art Nouveau*, as above, p.20

8   Polak, Ada, *Modern Glass*, London, 1962, p.82

9   Kaplický quoted in Frantz, *Contemporary Glass*, as above, p.38. Original from Josef Raban, 'The work of Josef Kaplický', *Czechoslovak Glass Review*, vol.17, no.8, 1962, p.231

10 Littleton, Harvey, 'Artist-Produced Glass: A Modern Revolution', paper delivered to the 8th International Congress on Glass, London. Quoted in Frantz, *Contemporary Glass*, as above, p.61

11 Cummings, Keith, 'Glass Making and the Evolution of the Craft Process', *The Persistence of Craft, the applied arts today*, Paul Greenhalgh, ed., A&C Black, London, 2002, pp.73–83

12 Jacquard, Max, *Clifford Rainey: The Savage Approach*; British Artists in Glass, Journal no.1, Spring 1989, p.25

13 See entry for Ann Robinson, p.112

14 'Flexible drive equipment consists of an electric motor, coupled to a flexible cable, at the end of which is a handpiece into which can be fitted a great variety of abrasive burrs and wheels.' For this and further explanation see Goodearl, Marilyn and Tom, *Engraved Glass, International Contemporary Artists*, Antique Collectors' Club, 1999, pp.19–20

15 See [9] above

Note to reader

Contemporary International Glass

The list of artists whose work is illustrated has been limited to works made after 1990. There follows a list of all other glass artists whose work since 1965 is in the collections.

Selection has been unavoidable owing to lack of space and I apologize that, inevitably, some artists have been omitted.

Only international solo exhibitions and international awards are listed (i.e., other than in the artist's home or adopted country) with the exception of the following.

- Coburg Glass Prize
- Glass Art Society (GAS) lifetime award
- Jerwood Prize for Glass
- Rakow Commission, Corning Museum of Glass

The following two mixed exhibitions are listed as an indication of international recognition.

- *Venezia Aperto Vetro*, Venice, 1996 and 1998
- *The Glass Skin*, Hokkaido Museum of Modern Art, Sapporo and touring to Shimonoseki and Gifu museums, Japan; Corning Museum of Glass, USA and Kunstmusuems, Düsseldorf and Coburg, Germany, 1997–99

The following British mixed exhibition is included as an indication of national recognition at a key moment in British glass.

- *The Glass Show: Contemporary British Glass*, Crafts Council, London and touring, 1993

Danny Lane

1955 Born Urbana, Illinois, USA

Balustrade

Float glass, cut and drilled, and steel
London, 1992
Height of each column 114cm
V&A: C.249-1993
Float glass made and donated by
Pilkington Glass
Commissioned for the V&A Glass Gallery

I set out to design something uncluttered and simple, I wanted the latent energy of the glass to speak for itself. I think the balustrade offers a strong contrast and counterpoint to the exhibits on display – 4,000 years of painstaking craftsmanship.

DL, quoted in Catherine Chester-Levy, 'Alighting on Glass', *Sotheby's Preview***, October, 1994**

Other works in the V&A's collection

V&A: C.193-1991 Chair
V&A: C.12:1,2 to C.13:1,2-2003 Two goblets and stands

Peter Aldridge

1947 Born Carshalton, Surrey, England

Artist's statement

I work with light in much the same way a musician uses sound. The underlying mathematical progression of individual notes, the multiplicity of overlaying rhythms, tonal range and chromatic intervals all have their parallels when composing with light.

The objects I make have an inherent mathematical progression, just as a musical instrument has proportion in its fingerboard and precision in its construction, both critical to the sound it produces.

In developing this language of visual harmonics, certain combinations of measurement are more visually acceptable than others. In the same manner musical intervals affect the ear, intervals of light affect the eye.

The pure geometry of light necessitates an extraordinary medium to bring out the subtleties of its visual energy. The transparency of glass, and in particular the purity of Steuben crystal, exemplifies this unique ability to internalize light. Indeed, this is the only material with a visual inner dimension, affording the sculptor insight into the very essence of things, transcending formal aesthetic convention. The constant movement and slight shifts in the frequencies that make up visible light pose mystery and paradox and are rich in metaphor.

PA, excerpt from an undated statement

A Moment in Time

Starphire glass, cut, polished, dichroic coatings, assembled
Corning, USA, 1998
Height 300cm
V&A: C.112:1-22-1998

Training

1964–66 Sutton School of Art, foundation course

1966–68 Hammersmith College of Art, London, BA(Hons)

1968–71 Royal College of Art, London, MA Glass, Sculpture

Professional/international

1971 Set up PSA-Design

1977 Artist-in-residence, Steuben Glass, USA; Sculpture centrepiece, UK Delegation to the European Space Agency; Coburg Glass Prize, honorary award, Germany

1978 'Peace Crystals' given by President Carter to President Sadat and Prime Minister Begin on the signing of the peace treaty between Israel and Egypt

1981–86 Senior design consultant, Steuben Glass

1983 National Endowment for the Arts Visual Artists Fellowship

1986 *National Steel* sculpture, Nippon Kokan, Tokyo HQ; executive director of Design, Corning Glassworks

1993 Sculpture installation, Corning Inc. World HQ

1996–2000 Vice President, Creative Director, Steuben Glass, Corning Inc.

2000 Sculpture, *Fantasia 2000*, Walt Disney Pictures, for Millenium celebration, New York, London, Paris, Tokyo, Los Angeles

2002 Creative director, 'Prominence Corp', Winter Olympics, Salt Lake City, Utah

2003 Principal, Peter Aldridge Design

Teaching

1972–78 Visiting professor and external examiner, Royal College of Art

1993–96 Senior tutor, head of Glass, Royal College of Art, London

Margaret Alston

1956 Born Liverpool, England

Artist's statement

Ideas as well as technique are of equal importance to my work. Technique can suggest the overall effect of a piece, but the form and decorative content may be inspired by such diverse sources as textiles, architecture and calligraphy. Age and antiquity are key references. The qualities and the associations of aged and worked objects whether man-made, such as ancient jewellery and architecture, or natural, such as fossils and stones such as jade, alabaster, granite and quartz, convey feelings which are fundamental elements of my work.

MA, 1993

Vase, **Indigo**, from the **Growth** series
Pâte de verre, incised
Bradford on Avon, England, 1992
Height 15cm
Gift of Paul Bedford
V&A: C.68-1994
Exhibited, *The Glass Show: Contemporary British Glass*, Crafts Council, 1993

Training
1978–79 Trent Polytechnic, Nottingham, foundation course

1979–83 North Staffordshire Polytechnic, Stoke-on-Trent, BA (Hons 1st class)

1979–84 Multi-disciplinary Design

1979–85 Royal College of Art, London, MA, Glass & Ceramics

Professional/international
1993 *The Glass Show*, London

1996 *Venezia Aperto Vetro*, invited artist

Teaching
1986–88 Part-time lecturer, Sunderland Polytechnic

1992 Part-time lecturer, Buckingham College

Galia Amsel

1968 Born London, England

Critical comment

[Galia Amsel's] work is executed in a number of techniques and processes from blowing to various casting methods including lost-wax, as demanded by the developing ideas and character of each piece. Objects are themselves the inspiration for her work, machines and moving parts and things that are functional as well as being both sculptural and decorative such as ritual and ethnic jewellery. It is the challenge of making individual and independent sculptural objects that still suggests the character of the original form whilst being translated into a language like glass that excites her.

Michael Robinson, *New Light: Recent work by four contemporary glass artists*, The Solomon Gallery, Dublin, 1996

Cast glass can be transparent or opaque or both at once and over the years she has learnt how to use these qualities to find inner spaces or what she refers to as 'revelations. There is a respect for ritual and for things that are made for a purpose. 'I like things that work – machinery, bridges, things that fit together and move, work together.'

Dan Klein, 'Galia Amsel: passage to a space beyond', *International Glass* no. 4/Object 40, 2002

Pierce 4

Cast clear lead glass with sandblasted texture; lost-wax cast blue glass cone insert, ground and polished
London, England, 1999
Length 57.5cm
Gift of Paul Bedford
V&A: C.56:1,2-1999

Training

1985–86 Loughton College of Further Education, foundation course

1986–89 Middlesex Polytechnic, Barnet, BA (Hons 1st class), 3-D Design

1989–91 Royal College of Art, London, MA, Glass & Ceramics

Professional/international

1993 Set up workshop, London; *The Glass Show*, London

1996 *Venezia Aperto Vetro*, invited artist

1999 Clara Scremini Gallery, Paris

2001 The Bullseye Connection Gallery, Portland, Maine, USA

2002 Clara Scremini Gallery, Paris

2004 Moves to New Zealand

Teaching

1992–95 Visiting lecturer at Glasgow School of Art, Staffordshire University, Stoke-on-Trent, Edinburgh School of Art

1996–98 Visiting lecturer, University of Sunderland

Other works in the V&A's Collection

V&A: C.64:1,2-1994 *Winding Journey*

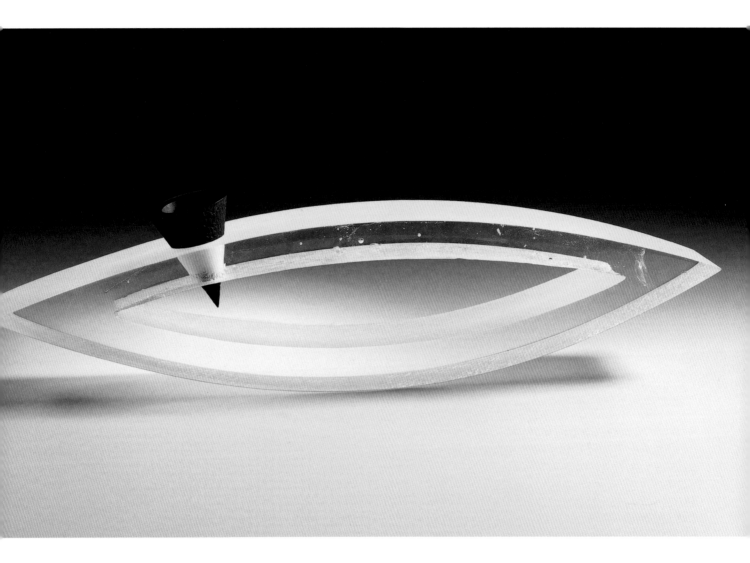

Dale Chihuly

1941 Born Tacoma, USA

Critical comment

Dale Chihuly is the best known and most visceral of glass artists. He has played an internationally formative part in establishing glass as a material for contemporary artists. He talks about translucency and brilliance of colour, as well as more and bigger glass. Yet his *Macchia*, *Baskets*, *Basket Sets*, *Persians* and *Persian Sets*, have each a particular dynamism and their breath-filled forms also have a compelling quality which is unsettling. In the V&A's collections, the darkest of them, the *Persian Set*, both attracts and menaces.

Chihuly's *Persians* series evolved from the *Seaforms* series in 1985 with experimental sessions by glass-blower, Martin Blank, under Chihuly's direction. Originally reminiscent of the tiny core-formed bottles of ancient Egypt and Persia, the series developed into a range of widely differing shapes, the outer container forms often of enormous size. These pieces are each decorated with lines of thin, trailed glass, the piece then blown into a ribbed mould leaving the 'spines' of thicker glass and then fully blown to shape. The outer form was spun out into a huge disk before being finally shaped by gravity and manipulating by hand. The *Persians* series, particularly when this darkly foreboding blue is set against the strident yellow, can be some of Chihuly's more aggressive and disturbing works.

JHO, unpublished text for *Beyond the Glass Gallery*, V&A, 2002

Although the natural beauty of glass is easily exploited, the use of its transformational properties is rarely attempted by artists who work in the medium. Chihuly is a master in the creation of transformational spaces through the construction of a *mise-en-scène*. The sources of his *Persians* are classical Greek, Persian, Byzantine, Islamic, Venetian and Art Nouveau, together representing an incredibly fertile palimpsest of ideas and influences. Yet for Chihuly, the *Persians* are only one expression of the underlying, purely abstract and formal objective of his work: the exploration of form and the glass itself as a vehicle for colour; and the orchestration of colour to create transformational environments.

Tina Oldknow, *Chihuly: Persians*, Portland Press, 1997, p.22

'In the beginning, the Persians had to do with the contrast between two colours…between open and closed forms…and the intensity of the body wraps.'
('Body wrap' is Chihuly's term for the stripe of colour applied to the body of the piece.)

Tina Oldknow, *Chihuly: Persians*, Portland Press, 1997, p.7

Deep Blue and Bronze Persian Set

Blown glass
Seattle, USA, 1999
Width 89cm
Acquired with assistance from the National Art Collections Fund and Paul Bedford
V&A: C.108:1-8-2001
Exhibited, *Chihuly at the V&A*, 2001

Training

1966–67 University of Wisconsin, Littleton glass program; M.S. Sculpture

1967 LC Tiffany Foundation Grant, Glass

1968 Fulbright Scholarship

Professional/international

1979 Museu de Arte de São Paulo, Brazil

1986–88 Musée des Arts Décoratifs, Paris

1990 Azabu Museum of Arts & Crafts, Tokyo, Japan; Museo Nacional de Bellas Artes, Santiago, Chile

1991 Prague, Umeleckoprumsylové muzeum, Czech Republic

1996 Distinguished Achievement Award, University of Washington, College of Arts & Sciences, Seattle, Washington

Innumerable exhibitions internationally each year, including among the more recent: *Chihuly over Venice*, Italy, 1996; *Chihuly in the Light of Jerusalem 2000*, Israel, 1999; *Chihuly at the V&A*, London, 2001

Teaching

1969–79 Established RISD and taught glass and sculpture courses

1971 Co-founder, Pilchuck Glass School, Washington State, and visiting-teaching at Pilchuck for 20 years

Continuous training for all assistants in the Chihuly workshops; establishment of teaching programmes for young people and seniors.

Other works in the V&A's collection

V&A: C.108-1979 *Basket*; C.203:A-C-1985 *Sea Form*; C.111:A-G-1987 *Davy's Gray Sea Form Set with Black Lip Wraps*; C.107-2001 *Kyoto Orange Macchia with Tar Lip Wrap*; C.109:1-5-2001 *Secret Garden Green Basket set with Black Lip Wraps*

Václav Cigler

1929 Born Vsetin, Czechoslovakia (now Czech Republic)

Artist's statement

Václav Cigler apprehends a shape in sketch drawings with flexible lines; these lines penetrating space embrace the volumes and surfaces of plastic models. He realizes the forms themselves in a wide range of expressions, starting from diminutive jewellery…and culminating with sculptural objects made from cut optical glass which pay homage to the pure beauty of the geometrical alphabet. Exactness and balance are qualities of his monumental compositions. With large volumes and a constructive conception of transparent and coloured glass material… these compositions become spatial. His spatial projects, an integral part of his work, form a kindred group. The spatial projects transform fragments of land and natural elements, and thus reach cosmic space. The human being and the space of his or her existence is the basis for his daring artistic efforts.

Jiří Šetlík, 'Space Light Glass', *Form Light Glass*, **Prague Castle, Prague and American Craft Museum, New York, 1995**

Space…What is space for me? A condition? An excuse? Both. It is mainly a medium of communication: physical…psychical…psychological… Space is a domain of energy, of intercepting stations, of the destiny of intersections…real ones or suggested ones. Space is a site of activities, i.e., of relationships. The sacred emptiness of space is not the emptiness of fulfilment but of accomplishment. This accomplishment is to be realized by means agreeable to both an intended effect, as well as to environmental character.

VC, *Form Light Glass*, **Prague Castle, Prague and American Craft Museum, New York, 1995**

Vejce (Egg: sign of secret and new life)

Cast optical glass, acid-polished and glued
Nový Bor (studio of Jan Frydrych), Czech Republic, made 2003
Length 32cm
Gift of the artist via Galerie Pokorna
V&A: C.181-2003
Vejce was first made in 1995; this is the third. Each is newly worked and different, i.e., original.

Training

1948–51 School of Professional Glass-making, Nový Bor

1951–57 Academy of Applied Arts, Prague (with Professor Josef Kaplický)

Professional/international

1979–present Independent artist in Bratislava, Czechoslovakia (now Slovakia)

Many international exhibitions including among the more recent: Museum um Boymans um Beuningen, Rotterdam; Gallery Am Graben, Vienna; SM Gallery E Gottschalk, Frankfurt; Kunstmesse, Maastricht; Rob van den Doel, The Hague

Teaching

1965–79 Lecturer and Director of Glass and Architecture Studio, Academy of Fine Arts, Bratislava

Tessa Clegg

1946 Born London, England

Critical comment

The first works in the new vein were shown in Venice in the *Aperto Vetro* of autumn 1996…still the vessel, but here was an exploration of the character and relationship of the vessel by contrasting it with quite different forms, one within the other. In these 'Play Boxes' a sharply perfect red square was placed in close confinement within a relaxed, soft, circular enclosing yet open form…Since then she has explored the possibilities of function and containment still further. The forms are yet more sculptural and abstract; the words 'minimal' and 'contemporary' have entered Clegg's own descriptions of her work. Moving on…to the series entitled *Arco* she now explores hidden space, defining it with colour – red continues to be a favourite – and in almost entirely enclosing the coloured shape she also defines transparency, internal and external volumes. Texture is used to describe the surface and to articulate the play of light and shadow on the glimpsed shape within.

JHO, 1996

The conceptual clarity of these new works arises from Clegg's incisive approach combined with an in-depth knowledge of her medium. Her judgement is clearly unclouded by the more seductive charms of glass. Instead, she is inclined to question critically why it is that so many glass artefacts, both craft and industrially produced, demonstrate only a narrow range of the material's potential – why it is that certain qualities such as clarity and brilliance seem to predominate. She sees glass as a highly versatile medium that can be worked to yield nearly limitless possibilities in compositions of colour, texture and form.

Tessa Peters, *Tessa Clegg*, Barrett Marsden Gallery, 2001

Artist's statement

In the last five years my work has changed and developed dramatically. In 1993, I was still involved in the concept of timeless beauty. It was the end of a long apprenticeship. I had invented for myself the glass-making process, kiln-formed glass-casting, and was ready to express that mastery. I began to make more sculptural, abstract forms. Minimal and contemporary in concept, they relate to hidden space, colour, transparency, light and shadow, and internal and external volumes. Always vessels, but a play on function and containment.

TC, *The Jerwood Prize for Applied Arts 1998: Glass*, Crafts Council, 1998, p.18

Arco 4
Lost-wax cast glass, ground and polished
London, 1998
Length 47cm
V&A: C.114:1,2-1998
Exhibited, *A Celebration of Glass*,
Contemporary Applied Arts Gallery, 1997

Training
1979–83 Stourbridge College of Art, BA (Hons) 3-D Design (under Keith Cummings q.v.)

Professional/international
1985, 1989, 1992 Galerie L, Hamburg, Germany

1988 Compositions Gallery, San Francisco

1990, 1996, 1998, 2000 Clara Scremini Gallery, Paris

1991 Sanske Gallery, Zurich, Switzerland

1993 *The Glass Show*, London

1995, 1996, 1998 Clara Scremini Gallery, Paris

1996 *Venezia Aperto Vetro*, invited artist

1998 Jerwood Prize for Glass, London

1999 Galerie von Bartha, Basel, Switzerland

1999, 2002 Barry Friedman Gallery, New York

Teaching
1984–92 Part-time lecturer, West Surrey College of Art & Design, Farnham

1992–98 Part-time lecturer, Middlesex University, London

1996–98 Artistic & Technical Director, North Lands Creative Glass, Caithness, Scotland

1992–2001 Part-time and associate lecturer, Royal College of Art, London

Other works in the V&A's collection
V&A: C.145-1993 Bowl
V&A: C.18-1995 Bowl

Deborah Cocks

1958 Born Sydney, Australia

Artist's statement

Splicing is a piece that evolved as I worked. I started with the fish. Fish are just wonderful to play with. They move, writhe, change and are so 'human'. They are the crowd rushing along regardless. These fish start to change as they get closer to the surface. Baubles appear on their fins and they turn into vessels. (Here it may be said that I have a concern about genetic modification.) As they break through the rope they gather passengers. With the humans one shows concern and shouts, the other seems to be quite enjoying the ride. Yes, that funny animal is based on the kangaroo, albeit stylized. The dog is our dog, Mustard, rabbits (introduced) run wild around here and there has to be a rooster in there somewhere because that is my name! Moths fly away and apples look the same, but are they really? The title comes from rope and gene splicing and was named by my partner Andrew Stewart when I explained the above story to him. Sometimes it takes someone else to put it together succinctly. While making and juxtaposing images I am hopefully leaving the narrative open to many interpretations. I'm fascinated to hear the viewers' thoughts. Often they are far more intriguing than the original intent. If it appears light-hearted and humorous, then well and good as being able to laugh is very important.

DC, 2004

Splicing

Slumped, painted in enamels and engraved
Brays Creek, Australia, 2004
Diam. 58.5cm
V&A: C.6:1,2-2004
Exhibited: *COLLECT*, Crafts Council, V&A, 2004

Training

Australian National University, BA (Fine Arts)

1984–5 Sydney College of the Arts, Graduate Diploma in Visual Arts (Glass) (under Maureen Cahill)

Professional/international

1986 Cocks & Blum Glass Workshop, Sydney

1987 Ausglass (Association of Australian Glass Artists) Conference: Gerhard Emmerich's glass painting workshop

1987, 1988 Scholarships to Pilchuck Glass School, USA (under Flora Mace and Joey Kirkpatrick, Ronald Pennell and Jiří Harcuba)

1988–90 Hancock and Cocks Glass Workshop, Sydney

1992 Set up workshop with potter Andrew Stewart, Brays Creek, NSW

Teaching

1990 Tutor, University of Western Sydney

1991 Visiting artist, University of New England, Northern Rivers campus (UNENR), Lismore, NSW (now the Southern Cross University)

Bob Crooks

1965 Born London, England

Critical comment

Bob Crooks has ebullient skills as a glass-blower, a willingness to take risks and effervescent enthusiasm. When I talked to him first he was about to set off for Pakistan and was full of plans for new shapes – something completely different. His restlessness and energy is reflected in his glassmaking…impatient and enthusiastic, his strengths are in instant production and a rapid turnover of ideas. His glass is immediate, glittering and attention-seeking.

JHO, 'A Celebration of Glass', *Crafts*, no. 153, July/August, 1998, p.30 and '50 Years of Craft', *Contemporary Applied Arts*, 1998, p.66

Artist's statement

The material drives my imagination, its changing possibilities and its metamorphic qualities, refraction and reflection, transparency and opacity, softness and sharpness: energetically working with its hot fluidity and changing qualities through cold processes…[*Winter Chrysalis*] has been developed especially for Venezia Aperto Vetro 1998. It is confident and demands a reaction to the forms and diverse exploitation of the material's properties: combining distorted mould-blown with free-blown elements and creating visual distortion through cutting and faceting alongside free-blown vessels using Venetian techniques; the differing thicknesses of the glass dictate the final form. Inspired by the ever-changing world around us, elements are subtracted from this and in turn amalgamated with others to form a whole.

BC, *International New Glass*, *Venezia Aperto Vetro*, Venice, 1998, p.66

Winter Chrysalis/ Chrysalis Winter
Blown, cased glass, cut and faceted, with applied spikes
London, England, 1998
Length 90cm
Gift of the artist
V&A: C.55-2002
Exhibited, *Venezia Aperto Vetro*, Venice; *Bob Crooks – Glass, Crafts Council Showcase*, V&A, 2000

Training
1984–5 Humberside College of Higher Education, foundation course

1985–9 West Surrey College of Art & Design, Farnham, BA (Hons), 3-D Design with Glass

Professional/international
1986–87 Assistant to resident Master glass-maker (Ronnie Wilkinson) at The Glasshouse, Covent Garden, London

1990–93 First Glass workshop, Newent, Gloucestershire.

1991 Contemporary Art Centre, Schalkwijk, The Netherlands

1993 Galerie Tessel, Den Burg, The Netherlands; *The Glass Show*, London

1994–2002 First Glass Partnership, Clapham, London

1998 *Venezia Aperto Vetro*, invited artist

2002 Moves First Glass workshop to Thelbridge, Devon

Teaching
1990–92 Part-time lecturer, University of Wolverhampton

1993–2002 Part-time lecturer, Buckingham College of Higher Education (Brunel University)

Other works in the V&A's collection
V&A: C.70-1994 candlestick
V&A: C.71-1994 wineglass

Keith Cummings

1940 Born London, England

Artist's statement

This is one of a series which take as their inspiration fragments and residues left by summer flowering, still in evidence in autumn and winter when the smallest area of richness and colour shows up. An essential part of this is the role played by material and process and the excitement and risks involving new experimental additions to the procedures. I feel very much part of an English tradition of landscape imagery.

KC, 19 December 1999

…my choice and development of kiln-formed glass as a primary method of creating form and assembling it with cast bronze and fabricated metal sections…has enabled me to create a drawn-out, many-staged process within which many opportunities present themselves for creative feed-back. Possible new formal directions are spread across many processes from wax to final assembly…I realize that I often deliberately court this process by delaying decisions to allow for maximum evolutionary change to occur…Klee's statement that 'formation is more important than form' has always seemed particularly true to me…In adopting a method that is long drawn out, complex and slow, I gain a creative process that suits me, but…I produce only a few pieces a year.

KC, from Andrew Brewerton, 'Something Rich & Strange; the Kiln-worked Glass of Keith Cummings', *Neues Glas/New Glass* 1/99, pp.28–35, original in *Point*, no. 3, Winter 1996, p.52

Windfall

Kiln-cast with metals (copper, bronze, silver and gold)
Wolverhampton, England, 1998
Length 26cm
V&A: C.1-2000
Exhibited, *Jerwood Prize for the Applied Arts: Glass*, Crafts Council and touring, 1998

Training

1958–62 University of Durham, BA (Hons) Fine Art (Painting, under Victor Pasmore and Richard Hamilton) and Glass Technology

Professional/international

1963 Architectural glass designer, Whitefriars Glass Co.

1983 Consultant designer, Stevens & Williams/Royal Brierley, glass, lighting and domestic ware

1984 Clara Scremini Gallery, Paris

1993 *The Glass Show*, London

1996 *Venezia Aperto Vetro*, invited artist

Teaching

1964–67 Lecturer in Art History, Blackpool School of Art

1967–86 Senior lecturer in Glass, Stourbridge College of Art & Technology

1974–85 Visiting lecturer and examiner, Ceramics & Glass Department, Royal College of Art, London

1986–93 Professor of Glass Studies, University of Wolverhampton

1994–present Reader in Research Studies, University of Wolverhampton

Other works in the V&A's collection

V&A: C.222-1987 *Mariner II*

Bernard Dejonghe

1942 Born Chantilly, France

Critical comment

The work of Bernard Dejonghe can be regarded as part of a creative tradition that reaches back to the Land Art of the 1970s, and is found today in sculpture as diverse as Andy Goldsworthy's fragile lyricism and James Turrell's monumental carving of the Arizona Desert…However… Dejonghe's vision is very much his own. His work in clay and latterly in glass connects strongly with the rugged Alpine landscape near Nice where he lives and works. Here is a place where forms are brought into focus by a searching light and where the bright mirror of mountain streams adds to the air's clarity…Dejonghe's forms seem to be as much about continually changing rhythms and movements, as of stasis and permanence…He uses virtuoso combinations of the optical and the opaque – rich seams and sections devitrified by complex firing and cooling processes…For Bernard Dejonghe this 'fusion of materials' is intriguing because both clay and glass are ancient substances, but remain central to the technology of our own time. His own use of this technology is an essential part of his dialogue with nature. Thus sculpture, exhilarating to behold in any interior, but ideally seen under the deep filter of a broad sky, has the visual power that recalls the megalithic structures of ancient man. Yet it also has a transient poetry as fresh and ethereal as an Alpine stream.

David Whiting, from *Bernard Dejonghe: ceramics & glass*, Galerie Besson, 1998

De connu en inconnu, la sculpture de Bernard Dejonghe nous entraîne dans cette relation étrange qu'elle instaure avec un lieu par sa présence, moments d'équilibre à découvrir, à vivre.

Corps et regard solicités, pour un au-delà de la rencontre d'une matière et d'une forme saisies par la fusion où gestes et pensées créent l'événement.

Manifestation de création, énergie en suspens, l'oeuvre ne cesse de s'aventurer.

From known to unknown, Bernard Dejonghe's sculptures, through their very presence, lead us into this strange relationship that they establish with a place, moments of balance to discover and to experience.

Both the body and gaze are sought after to go beyond the junction of a material and a form caught by fusion, where gestures and thoughts create the event.

It is a manifestation of creation and, like suspended energy, the work never stops venturing forward.

Jacqueline Lerat, from *Bernard Dejonghe: Siliciums Nuages Clairs*, Chateau d'Eau & Maison de Culture, Bourges, 2000, p.7 (original French and translation)

Petit Phrase

Kiln-cast, devitrified areas, and hand-chiselling
Briançonnet (Alpes-Maritime), 1996
Height 25cm
V&A: C.109-1998
No. 5 from a vocabulary of seven forms shown in Musée d'Evreux, 1996 as *Petit Phrase avec Saturne*.
Exhibited, *Bernard Dejonghe: ceramics & glass*, Galerie Besson, 1998

Training
1960–64 Ecole des Métiers d'Art de Paris

Professional/international
1969–76 Ceramic workshop at Fontenay-aux-Roses (formerly Emile Decoeur's workshop)

1976 Builds present studio at Briançonnet

1986 Began work in glass

1992 La Neuveville, Switzerland

1995 Musée Bellerive, Zürich

1996 Galerie De Witte Voet, Amsterdam; *Venezia Aperto Vetro*, guest of honour

1997–99 *The Glass Skin*, invited artist, Japan

1998 Etela Karjatan Art Museum, Lappeenranta, Finland; Galerie Besson, London

1999 Galerie B, Baden-Baden, Germany

Anna Dickinson

1961 Born London, England

Critical comment

Anna Dickinson's sculptural vessels change in small increments. The work cannot be described as 'improving' because it has always seemed perfect in design and execution. For Dickinson, fabricating the objects herself is inseparable from their essence, purpose and value. The glass is blown, cut, sandblasted, and/or engraved, then electro-formed with various metals, including silver and copper. The metalwork is understated and usually given a restrained finish. Beyond decoration, it suggests structural integration into the architecture of the vessels. Through these works Dickinson acknowledges the influences of African and Latin American wood carvings, basketry, and textiles, as well as the ceramics of Hans Coper and Lucie Rie.

Susanne K Frantz, *Neues Glas/New Glass* **2/98, pp.104–5**

Some artists trade in certainties. Technique is the key: the skilled ability to coax a material into speaking the right language, controlled reliably and repeatedly. Beyond that, the characteristic handling of the chosen material, a distinctive palette, a close group of favoured images and a personality which confirms well-established expectations. Anna Dickinson has the skills to make glass speak for her. She has a vocabulary which is hers alone. Other artists challenge, other artists shock, this artist affirms and enriches.

JHO, *Anna Dickinson,* **Galerie von Bartha, Basel, 2001, p.5**

Vase

Mitre-cut, with electro-formed gold rim
London, England, 1998
Height 45cm
Gift of Paul Bedford
V&A: C.111-1998
The blank blown by Neil Wilkin to Anna Dickinson's design

Training

1977–79 Hounslow Borough College, London, foundation course

1979–82 Middlesex Polytechnic, London, BA 3-D Design, Glass and Metal

1983–85 Royal College of Art, London, MA, Glass

Professional/international

1991 Koyanagi Gallery, Tokyo

1993 Kurokabe Glass Museum, Nagahama, Japan; *The Glass Show,* London

1996 *Venezia Aperto Vetro,* guest of honour

1997, 2001, 2002 Galerie von Bartha, Basel, Switzerland

Other works in the V&A's collection

V&A: C.243-1986 Bowl
V&A: C.37-1994 Vase
V&A: C.3,4,5,6,7-2001 hair ornaments for Romeo Gigli

Erwin Eisch

1927 Born Frauenau, Germany

Critical comment

The source of Erwin Eisch's art has always been the spontaneous gesture, the immediate reaction to a creative spark. Actually this is a typical approach for a painter, and that is how Eisch primarily saw himself for a long time. But he comes from a glass-making region and a glass-making family. And there were sculptors among his ancestors. Thus, a unique interrelationship of painting, glass, and sculpture – sometimes, almost a love-hate relationship – is present in his work.

Helmut Ricke, 'Erwin Eisch', *The Glass Skin***, Hokkaido Museum of Modern Art, 1997 p.48**

Artist's statement

'Break through the wall' – this theme I have used for the second time to express my feeling about this most important event which happened in Berlin, November 1989. At that time Helmut Kohl was the German Chancellor, so I used his portrait, a glass head, for this theme. The wall that divided the city was a symbol of stupidity, of fear and the escaping people were searching, running for freedom, peace and to become human beings. I am using my glass heads and portraits as a three-dimensional canvas, searching for images, messages.

EE, 2004

Helmut Kohl: Break Through the Wall

Mould-blown, painted, gilded and sandblasted
Frauenau, Germany, model made 1997; blown 2002, painted 2003–4
Height 43cm
Gift of the artist
V&A: C.5-2004

Training

1946–9 Apprenticeship, glass-engraving in workshop of father, Valentin Eisch

1949–52 Academy of Fine Arts, Munich, glass-engraving

1957 Introduction to hot glass

1956–59 Academy of Fine Arts, Munich, sculpture

Professional/international

1960 Founded art group Radama, with Max Strack and Gretel Stadler

1962 Met Harvey Littleton (see *Introduction*); set up glass studio in Frauenau

1977, 1985 Coburg Glass Prize, honorary award, first prize

1982, 1995 Glass Art Society, Honorary Life Membership and Lifetime Achievement Award, USA

1992 Kristallnacht Project, Gold Award for *My Love to Anne Frank*, American Interfaith Institute, Philadelphia; *The Glass Skin*, Japan

Teaching

Various guest professorships in USA and Europe

1988–present Summer school Bild-Werk Frauenau, teaching and painting

Bohumil Eliáš

1937 Born Nasobůrky, Czechoslovakia (present-day Czech Republic)

Critical comment

Over a long career Bohumil Eliáš has explored a variety of different pathways, in materials, techniques and in ideas. Many Czech glass artists of his generation, and that of his teachers, have drawn upon western European art movements. Thus they crossed political boundaries but also, with the deliberate synthesis of the 'fine art' of painting with glass sculpture, they signalled the arrival of a new art form and gave glass an instant validity as an art material. Eliáš responded especially to Abstract Expressionist painting and for him, bringing the two together has some-times meant literally combining painted canvas with painted glass. He has worked on many architectural commissions and so he has a special familiarity with flat (window) glass and an interest in layering glass in small sculptures reminiscent of architectural models. As with *Gate*, here, he works in many different techniques including cutting in irregular shapes, painting in enamel colours, etching with acid and sandblasting. He has also fused sand and, on occasions, metal wire to the glass surface.

JHO, unpublished text for *Beyond the Glass Gallery*, V&A, 2002

Gate

Flat glass, cut, painted, with fused sand
Prague, Czech Republic, 1997
Height 100cm
Gift of the artist
V&A: C.113-1998
Exhibited, *Bohumil Eliáš: Glass Sculpture*,
Studio Glass Gallery, London, 1997

Training

1952–54 Training Institution of Glassmaking, Nový Bor

1954–57 Specialized School of Glassmaking, Zelezný Brod

1957–63 Academy of Applied Arts, Prague, (under Professor Josef Kaplický)

Professional/international

Innumerable exhibitions internationally each year including, among the most recent:

1990 Galerie Gottschalk-Betz, Frankfurt; Habatat Gallery, Michigan

1992 Galerie L, Hamburg; Galerie Carpe Diem, Paris; Gallery Nakama, Tokyo

1993 The Glass Art Gallery, Toronto

1994 Glass Art Gallery, Roeselare, Belgium

1997 The Studio Glass Gallery, London

1998 Habatat Galleries, Detroit

1999 Galerie Rob van den Doel, The Hague, The Netherlands; Abbaye Du Val St Lambert, Liège, Belgium; Galerie L, Hamburg

2001 Reykjavik Art Museum, Iceland

2002 Drammens Culturehouse, Norway

2003 Gallery Enomoto, Osaka, Japan; Habatat Gallery, Florida

Teaching

1984 Kent State University, Ohio, USA

Deborah Fladgate

1957 Born Nicosia, Cyprus

Critical comment

The maker Deborah Fladgate indicates with her small bowls how much subtlety of texture, surface and colour can be quietly wrought in cased, sandblasted, cut and fire-polished glass.

Marina Vaizey, 'Studio Glass', *Crafts*, no. 146, Jan/Feb 1994, p.54

Artist's statement

There are concerns that each piece of work has to fulfil; the form, the weight, the balance, the way a piece sits, the surface qualities and the way light is caught. I started working on the 'boat' series a couple of years ago and this theme has brought a more acute focus to my work. The *Reed Boat* involves extensive cutting and allows an exploration into the depths of glass letting light into the walls.

DF, *Glass UK: British Contemporary Glass*, National Glass Centre, Sunderland, 1998

Reed Boat

Blown, sandblasted, cut and polished
Leslie (Fife), Scotland, 1998
Length 33.1cm
Gift of Adrian Sassoon Esq
V&A: C.57-1999
Exhibited, *Glass UK: British Contemporary Glass*, National Glass Centre, Sunderland and *Fluid and Flat*, Cowdy Gallery, Newent, Gloucestershire, 1998

Training
1975–79 West Surrey College of Art & Design, BA (Hons) Ceramics

1980–82 Royal College of Art, London, MA, Glass

Professional/international
1979 Assistant, Anthony Stern Glass, London

1979–80 Assistant, Cowdy Glass Workshop, Gloucestershire

1980 Artist-in-residence, Wedgwood Glass, Norfolk

1981 Artist-in-residence, Dartington Crystal, Devon

1982 Assistant, Shirley Cloete, South Africa

1983 Established Fladgate Studio Glass, Farnham

1986 Set up workshop in Leslie, Fife, Scotland

1993 *The Glass Show*, London

Teaching
1979–80 and 1982–85 Part-time lecturer, Buckingham College of Higher Education

1983–84 Visiting lecturer, Royal College of Art, London

1984 Visiting lecturer, Sunderland Polytechnic

1984–86 Visiting lecturer, West Surrey College of Art & Design, Farnham

Ray Flavell

1944 Born Bilston, West Midlands, England

Critical comment

His style, as one might expect from someone trained in Scandinavia, is…controlled…A deep respect for the material and for glass-working techniques always shows in his work. He very often works in clear glass, and when he uses colour that too has a clarity about it. He is basically a vessel-maker, though he has also used vessel forms as elements in a series of sculptures that have poise and charm. His method of decorating the surface is usually by sandblasting. The colourless crystal bowls are treated with sandblasting and explore a fantasy world of light and imagery that at first looks familiar but on close scrutiny is lacking a known identity.

Dan Klein, *Glass, A Contemporary Art*, Collins, 1989, pp.147–8, and *British Studio Glass*, a Sunderland Arts Centre touring exhibition, 1983–4

Flavell's imagery is an imagined world of organic survival. He feels close to nature, to the blowing of the wind, the breaking of the waves and the hidden world of creatures and organisms that struggle for survival in the adverse conditions to which they are exposed. Since his move to Scotland his work reflects the harsher natural environment there, the rugged coastal areas and the lochs…the 'often ceaseless winds thrashing waves over rocks and yet creating a fecundity of coastal life in so doing'…He is fascinated by cosmic issues, 'space and time and that sort of thing', and is excited to think that there is still a lot for him to explore in that kind of imagery.

Dan Klein, *Ray Flavell, Neues Glas/New Glass*, no. 4, 1995, p.26

Artist's statement

I seek to investigate form, structure and surface to celebrate the particular qualities of glass. The pieces are derived from blown glass, often asymmetrical, forms. The tension of the forms [is] restated in the profile of the flat glass which also serves to orientate the two blown elements. I aim to retain the identity of the vessel, a traditional vehicle for both function and expression through the history of artefacts. The pieces are cut and polished to create depth and distortion to the sandblasted surfaces.

RF, *Contemporary British Glass*, Crafts Council, 1993

Greenpiece

Flat and blown, cut, sandblasted and assembled
Edinburgh, Scotland, 1991
Length 36.4cm
V&A: C.204-1991

Training

1960–64 Wolverhampton College of Art, N.D.D., Ceramics & Lithography

1965 Wolverhampton College of Art, product design

1968 Royal College of Art, London, one-year glass course (under Sam Herman)

1972 Orrefors Glass School, Sweden

1974–81 West Surrey College of Art & Design, BA (Hons), Glass

2000 Heriot-Watt University, PhD

Professional/international

1975–79 Consultant, Stevens & Williams/Royal Brierley Crystal

1985 Glass artist and designer to Jiva, Japan

1993 *The Glass Show*, London

1996 *Venezia Aperto Vetro*, guest of honour

Teaching

1966-87 Principal lecturer in Glass (formerly product design) West Surrey College of Art, Farnham

1980–85 Visiting tutor, Royal College of Art

1990– Course leader, Edinburgh College of Art, Glass & Architecture, Heriot-Watt University

Other works in the V&A's collection

V&A: C.100-1981 bowl, *Runes*
V&A: C.237-1986 bowl
V&A: C.107-1998 vase

Bert Frijns

1953 Born Kerkrade, The Netherlands

Critical comment

The work of Bert Frijns is best described as radically simple. He works with everyday window glass which he transforms by slumping it in a kiln. This is a technique that he has…brought to an unparalleled degree of refinement…allowing the glass to soften in a kiln and every now and then intervening in the process by introducing an indentation or by some other kind of manipulation. These are simple concepts which require great technical expertise born of long experience.

Venice, Comune di Venezia: *Venezia Aperto Vetro: International New Glass*, **1996, p.58**

What makes Frijns's works different from those of other artists is the absolute assurance with which he uses his formal means, especially his meticulously controlled kiln-shaping. Heated glass responds to pressure in the same manner as human skin; it gives way and it can be stretched. In this manner, works…communicate something organic and moving, despite their geometry of form and severity. For this artist, a minimal intervention always produces a maximal effect. This can be seen, for example, in the gradual, hardly perceptible descent of his objects… Frijns's works revolve around the concepts of balance and harmony, and this is most simply and clearly demonstrated in his vessel form that rests on a fraction of one square millimetre, thus requiring just the smallest push to result in instability and movement.

Helmut Ricke, *The Glass Skin*, **Corning Museum of Glass, New York, 1998, p.54**

For more than twenty years his raw material has been industrial 'plate-glass', the everyday window glass, available from any glass dealer in sheets of various sizes and thickness…The glass is heated at a temperature between 580 and 900°C and sags over supporting moulds without melting. Gradually the glass sheet wilts under its own weight into a droplet shape. The secret is to know exactly when to stop the heating process to attain a precise form. A few degrees can make an enormous difference. Frijns developed this apparently simple method…by…many years of trial and error and endows his work with astonishing precision, scale and quality…the flat landscape, the sea and the sky – all typically Dutch – create a natural grey and sharp light, which seems to reflect in his work…The silence of this extensive polder also echoes in his contemplative pieces…Though they resemble dishes, vases and bowls, they don't possess a specific function…he never uses colours, only the natural green tint of the window-pane, visible in the base, but especially at the top, where graphic circles contrast with the transparent silvery volumes.

Peter van Kester, 'Bert Frijns: the glass is half full', *Glass*, **no. 83, summer, 2001**

Balance
Slumped sheet glass
Haamstede, Zeeland, The Netherlands, 1999
Depth 34cm
Anonymous Gift
V&A: C.4:1-3-2000

Training
1973-80 Gerrit Rietveld Academy, Amsterdam, Sculpture department (1973–8); Glass department (1978–80)

Professional/international
1980–89 Independent workshop in Landsmeer

1988 *World Glass Now 88*, first prize, Hokkaido, Japan

1989–91 Work in Aulnay de Saintonge, France

1990, 1992 Musée des Arts Décoratifs, Lausanne, Switzerland

1991–present Independent workshop in Zeeland

1996 *Venezia Aperto Vetro*, guest of honour

1997 Musée-Atelier du Verre, Sars-Poteries, France

1997–99 *The Glass Skin*, invited artist, Japan

1998 Eretz Israel Museum, Tel Aviv, Israel

Gillies-Jones

Stephen Gillies, 1967 Born Halifax, West Yorkshire, England
Kate Jones, 1966 Born Hillingdon, Middlesex, England

Artist's statement

We have developed the form and its proportions using the horse-chestnut seed or 'Aesculus' as inspiration. The blown-glass vessel uses Swedish overlay to add layers of colour to the form, which is then removed through a process of sand carving to develop the surface pattern revealing the layers of colours and clear glass involved in the structure of the vessel. Each of the patterns is developed within a specific thematic concept, taking inspiration from scientific theory and elements of the landscape. ...[This is] an Aesculus Vessel, using red and transparent cobalt blue glass, exploring the rivers theme...the idea of the rivers on the planet operating as a balanced system, and how, with the rise of civilization and the damming of water in the western hemisphere, the weight of this contained water has tilted the earth on its axis. This relates to the notion that nothing happens in isolation, which is a recurrent theme of the surface-pattern imagery. This also relates to the mathematics of π, the golden mean...an awe-inspiring principle that the mathematics and structure of tree branches and roots of trees are the same system as a river system, as the blood vessels inside our bodies. All these theories are used as inspiration for the patterns on the work.

As contemporary glass-makers we take our context from the rich history of vessel-making and for us it is paramount to have the skills to realize our ideas. We specialize in the vessel form, and choose to celebrate its ability to transcend function and become a work of art.

G-J, 2003

Aesculus Bowl, Blue over Red,
from the **Rivers** series
Swedish overlay, wheel-cut and sandblasted
Rosedale, Yorkshire 2003
Depth 27.5cm
V&A: C.126-2003
Designed and sandblasted by Kate Jones, blown by Stephen Gillies, the form wheel-cut by Richard Lamming, Ruskin Glass Centre, Stourbridge, to Gillies-Jones's design.

Training
Stephen Gillies
1987–89 Stourbridge College of Art, BA (Hons) 3-D Glass Design, unfinished

1990–91 Wolverhampton University, BA (Hons) 3-D Glass Design

1991 Assistant, First Glass, Newent, Gloucestershire

1992 Glass-maker Ebeltoft Glass Museum, Denmark

1993–94 Assistant Baldwin-Guggisberg, Switzerland

Kate Jones
1984–85 Harrow College of Art, foundation course

1985–89 Stourbridge College of Art, BA (Hons) Fine Art

Professional/international
1993–2001 Stephen Gillies: assistant to various masters including Dale Chihuly, Lino Tagliapietra, Josiah McElheney, Jan Erik Ritzman, Richard Marquis

1994–present Gillies-Jones workshop, Rosedale, Yorkshire

Teaching
Stephen Gillies
1994 Visiting lecturer, International Glass Centre, Stourbridge

1998, 2001 Visiting lecturer and demonstrator, National Glass Centre, Sunderland

2001 Visiting lecturer, British Council, Crafts Council

Vincent van Ginneke

1956 Born Rotterdam, The Netherlands

Artist's statement

Sculptures which are constantly kissed – with worn feet, such as *pietàs* – both disconcert and move me. This boundless devotion people have for an image, be it the Virgin Mary or a fighter-plane, is fascinating.

Displayed in my workshop are shapes which I can only describe as memories of body-parts. Cross-sections through the waist, the transition into the legs, the gentle curve of the back.

Glass can easily become too beautiful and to polish it is very tempting, but with a matt skin, the outside shape becomes more important and you can work with contrasts. Once I made a work, which I had polished completely, matt again, just to force myself to focus on the essential.

V van G, extracts from *Beeld, Nederlandse Kring van Beeldhouwers*, (Dutch sculptors' association) 4-2003, supplement 24, p.2 (transl. R Liefkes)

Body Shape VI, one of 6
Lost-wax cast, part-polished
Almere, The Netherlands, 2003
Length 50cm
Anonymous Gift
V&A: C.10-2004
Exhibited, *Transparency*: a subtle play between the artists Michel Cleempoel (Belgium) impression, light, shadow, and Vincent van Ginneke (Netherlands) glass sculpture, Art-O-Nivo Gallery, Bruges, Belgium, 2003

Training
1972–77 Schoonhoven Technical School, The Netherlands, Master gold- and silver-smithing
1979–84 Gerrit Rietveld Academy, under Sybren Valkema, Mieke Groot (q.v.), Richard Meitner (q.v.)

Professional/international
1984–present Independent glass artist, workshop in Amsterdam
1995–present Independent glass artist, workshop in Almere, The Netherlands
1992, 2000 Galerie DM Sarver, Paris
1996 *Venezia Aperto Vetro*, invited artist
1999 Sars-Poteries, France
2003 Art-O-Nivo, Bruges, Belgium

Teaching
1991–present Workshops in Stoke-on-Trent Polytechnic, UK, Centro de Arte & Comunicação Visual, Almada, Lisbon, Hogeschool Limburg, Belgium, AKI Enschede, and Tetterode Glass-studio, Amsterdam
1994, 96, 97 Workshops in Atelier du Verre, Sars-Poteries, France
2000–present Gerrit Rietveld Academy, Glass Department

Mieke Groot

1949 Born Alkmar, The Netherlands

Critical comment

Mieke Groot is concerned with the vase as a timeless, 'classical' carrier of expression and meaning…The artist has placed all of her emphasis on the exterior, the shell of the undefined inner life. The enamel, applied in layers and fired in several stages, develops the cracked and torn structure that makes the objects so fascinating.

Helmut Ricke, *The Glass Skin*, Hokkaido, Museum of Modern Art, 1997, p.60

Ever in search of perfection, Mieke Groot intrigues anyone looking at her objects: a first impression of simplicity through the round, fluid, easy and universal forms changes to investigation upon seeing the thick, violent and cracked material of intense colour which seems perfectly mastered. The enamel is used as a sculptural material and seems to tell a story of warm countries which cannot leave us indifferent. Mieke Groot pushes the glass to its limits, far from its initial transparency by adding intense and perfectly mastered colours to give it a new personal expression …Mieke Groot does not seek the magical effect that glass can have. Glitter does not attract her greatly but she enjoys pushing glass to the limits of its use.

Anne Vanlatum, *15th Anniversary Celebration*, Braggiotti Gallery, 2002

Artist's statement

…My link with Djenné was my brother Caspar, who is a member of the restoration advisory committee [in Mali]. There he came into contact with traditional mud-brick building and he became an expert on the subject …Through research the engineers discovered that old dried-out clay shrank less than the new clay. In short, what had happened was that termites had eaten the straw. The insects left their droppings which caused a reaction with the material. This changed the characteristics of the clay and caused it to shrink much less. The engineers decided to add a percentage of the old material to the new – no straw this time…the material hardly shrank and therefore guaranteed the durability of the house. At that time I had developed pieces of work that has thick layers of enamel on the surface…during the firing process, the enamel would partly come off. Also the enamel skin was rather fragile after firing. As a result of the technical adventure of my brother in Djenné…I employed the same principle with my enamel. To the new enamel I added leftover enamel that had been mixed with water, sand and medium and which had, over a period of time, dried out…I achieved the results I needed.

MG, 'Behind Glass', transcript of a lecture given to the Glass Art Society conference, *Sources of Inspiration*, Amsterdam, 2002, pp.34–35

Untitled

Blown glass, dark red cased, with applied and fired enamel, mixed with sand
Amsterdam, 2002
Height 37cm
Anonymous Gift
V&A: C.37-2002
Exhibited, *15th Anniversary Celebration*, Braggiotti Gallery, Amsterdam, 2002

Training

1969–74 Gerrit Rietveld Academy, Amsterdam, Jewellery course

1974–76 Gerrit Rietveld Academy, Amsterdam, Glass course (under Sybren Valkema)

Professional/international

1976 Own glass studio with Richard Meitner

1979–82 Freelance designer, Royal Leerdam glassworks

1989–83 Board member of Fonds BK, Vormgeving en Bouwkunst

1993–94 Freelance designer, Sarner Cristal, Sarnen, Switzerland and Stolzle Oberglas, Barnbach, Austria

1984–95 Instructor, Summer School, Sars-Poteries, France

1995–present Advisor, Ernsting Stiftung Alter Hof Herding, Coesfeld-Lette, Germany

1997–99 *The Glass Skin*, Japan

1998 Workshop at North Lands Creative Glass, Lybster, Scotland

Teaching

1980–2000 Leader (with Richard Meitner), Gerrit Rietveld Academy glass course

1987–89 External Assessor, Royal College of Art, London

1996 Instructor with Frank van den Ham, Workshop, Instituto di Cultura, Aruba, West Indies

1995–97 Instructor Musée-Atelier du Verre, Sars-Poterie, France

Tony Hanning

1950 Born Traralgon, Victoria, Australia

Artist's statement

Dio is a self-portrait. The title, *Dio*, is short for diorama. Tony Hanning offers a lengthy statement on the many layers of meaning and intention within this complex work, an (inevitably unfairly) abbreviated version of which appears below.

The notion of the 'diorama' as a simulated environment is not so far removed from the glass vessel. In a diorama we see intersecting horizontal and vertical planes, which attempt to disguise themselves with a feeling of continuity; verticals (at the point at which they intersect with the horizontal) are meant to appear as if they continue on as horizontal planes. Mountains appear as painted images somehow connected to the horizontal and the sky…In *Dio*, however, drops or puddles of water lie taut on the horizontal planes and reflect the image of the mountains as if they were real…Gestural lines, seemingly serving no purpose, trail their way across the piece as if by accident, but closer inspection reveals that they cast shadows…The horizontal floors of each diorama cast shadows on the dioramas beneath them in the same way as clouds…There is…one diorama which appears relatively complete in that it is made up of images of mountains on the walls with a sphere somehow floating above the floor of the diorama. This floating sphere appears in most of the artist's major works and is a metaphor for 'self'. It is a signature of sorts.

This series of mind games and ambiguous statements, which is the hallmark of the artist's work, is further enhanced by the judicious use of shadows, suggesting a hierarchy of simulcra.

Tony Hanning, extracts from a statement accompanying the work, V&A records, 2002

Dio

Blown triple overlay, sandblasted
Yinnar, Australia, 2002
Height 36.5cm
Gift of Kirra Gallery, Australia
V&A: C.56-2002
The cased blank was blown by David Hay to
Tony Hanning's design

Training

1971–72 Gippsland Institute of Advanced Education, (Monash University), Diploma, Visual Arts

Professional/international

1972–81 Director, Latrobe Regional Gallery

1981 Set up Budgeree Glass partnership

1984 Working with Paul Marioni, Seattle, USA (Visual Arts Craft Board of the Australia Council travel grant)

1987–88 Studio in Byron Bay, New South Wales

1988 Glass Gallery, Bethesda, USA

1989–present Studios in Yinnar, then Morwell, Australia

Teaching

1970 Yallourn Technical College, Victoria

1987 Teacher/ assistant, Pilchuck Glass School, Washington State

1991 Central Gippsland College

Clare Henshaw

1964 Born Warwick, Warwickshire, England

Critical comment

…she cites Mark Rothko as being the greater influence on her work. She acknowledges the visionary calling of the British Romantic School, particularly the work of Cecil Collins (1908–89) whose symbolic, ethereal art also refused to obey the laws of gravity. Collins's influence is important and apparent, Rothko's far less so – although I can see his attraction for an artist working with glass, as his luminous spatial canvases float towards you. It is also interesting to be reminded that Rothko was once a surrealist, exploring psyche before devoting himself to his powerful abstract paintings. But it is Cecil Collins's dream fantasies, reincarnated in the hands of this young glass-engraver, that haunt us.

Ralph Turner, 'Heart of Glass', *Crafts*, vol.118, 1992, p.44

Artist's statement

Glass is a fluid material. Even when cooled and in 'solid' form, it is constantly moving. Behaving as does a liquid, it demonstrates that despite the outward appearance of things, all is temporal and transitory. Thus, for me, the medium of glass is a visible expression of the flow of life.

In the act of drawing and engraving an image, I aim to express the life and dynamism of that image; to depict matter as change. The images represent aspects of life, both dreamed and imagined. Archetypal figures and themes occur and recur throughout the work. The River, Bridges, Kings, Angels and the Trickster present themselves there.

Springing from the unconscious, the images themselves project the contents of the unconsciousness of the World. My objective is to ascribe consciousness to every expression of nature. With the discovery of our own imaginative possibilities we may participate in the imagination of the world. Entering a great cyclical flow of life, each thing, however small, is an essential participant totally interdependent on all other things.

CH, 1991

Visible Voices
Free-blown, cased glass, flexible wheel-engraved and sandblasted
Bristol, England, 1992
Height 26.2cm
Gift of the Alastair Pilkington Fund
V&A: C.230-1993
The cased (Swedish overlay technique) blank blown by Neil Wilkin to Claire Henshaw's design
Exhibited, *Clare Henshaw*, Jeanette Hayhurst Fine Glass, 1999

Training
1982–83 Herefordshire College of Art & Design, Dip. A.D.

1984–88 West Surrey College of Art & Design, BA (1st class Hons), 3-D Design, Glass

1988–90 Royal College of Art, London, MA, Ceramics & Glass

Professional/international
1985–86 Assistant to Ida Lochen and Peter Svarrer, Christiana Glaspusterie, Copenhagen, Denmark

1992 Timir Gallery, Amsterdam, The Netherlands

1993 *The Glass Show*, London

1996 Visiting artist, Australian National University, Canberra School of Art, Canberra

1998 Visiting artist, University of Industrial Arts, Helsinki, Finland

2001 Guest designer, Orrefors-Kosta Boda glassworks, Sweden

Teaching
1991–92 Lecturer, West Surrey College of Art & Design, Farnham

1996 Master Glass Workshop, engraving project with women at Mutijulu Aboriginal Community, Uluru, Northern Territories, Australia

1998 External assessor, University of Industrial Arts, BA glass and ceramics, Helsinki, Finland

Other works in the V&A's collection
V&A: C.38-1994 *The Marriage II*

Diana Hobson

1943 Born Stoke-on-Trent, England

Critical comment

In the *Language of Light* series, her work appears like poetry itself, made physical. It is haiku in glass, ceramics and stone, wood and bronze. Her sculpture is spare but eloquent. The images are archetypal, but the work seems intensely personal. It can be puzzling, but it is always understood.

Karen S Chambers, 'Diana Hobson: Speaking Clearly', *NeuesGlas/New Glass*, 1996, p.14

Artist's statement

–It is a beginning step towards unity.

–Only a first step?

–No. All things are present within a single moment.

–What do you mean?

–I mean that your final step is contained within your first. Life is a circle, the beginning is always the end.

DH, from 'Windhorse Woman', by Lynn V. Andrews, 'A conversation between Agnes Whistling Elk and her apprentice Lynn Andrews', quoted in *Language of Light*, Butler Gallery, 1996

'The transition piece from the earlier series of work 7 STEPS, 1990. Circles. The fragment holds the essence of the whole.'

DH, *Language of Light*, Dublin, 1996

Fragment of a Circle

Stone, bronze, silver and *pâte de verre*
London, England, 1990
Length 15cm
Gift of the Alastair Pilkington Fund
V&A: C.78:1-3-1996
Bronze cast by the Milton Keynes Bronze Foundry; stone found on the Derbyshire/Cheshire borders
Exhibited, *Seven Steps*, Los Angeles, 1990; *Language of Light*, Butler Gallery, Kilkenny Castle, 1996

Training

1958 Trainee designer for Clarice Cliff Ceramics

1959–64 Stoke-on-Trent School of Art, National Diploma in Design, Ceramics

1973–76 Royal College of Art, London, MA, Metals

1976–77 British Council Scholarship, The Atenaeum School of Art & Design, Helsinki, Finland

1988–90 Extended studies, Sir John Cass School, City of London Polytechnic, Sculpture

Professional/international

1965–71 Designer, Howard Pottery Ltd

1972–73 Enamellist to Wendy Ramshaw

1985 Coburg Glass Prize, 3rd prize, Germany

1990 Kurland Summers Gallery, Los Angeles, USA

1996 Butler Gallery, Kilkenny Castle, Ireland; *Venezia Aperto Vetro*, invited artist

2000 Artist-in-residence, Royal Botanic Gardens, Edinburgh; Edinburgh College of Art

2003 Working with video installation, Museum of Art & History, Santa Cruz, California, USA

Teaching

1979–87 Lecturer in metals, Camberwell School of Art & Crafts

1987–present Numerous teaching workshops in UK, Europe, Australia, Japan, USA

Other works in the V&A's collection

V&A: C.124-1994 bowl; V&A: C.109-1986 bowl; V&A: C.66-1994 bowl

Catherine Hough

1948 Born Bristol, England

Artist's statement

The making of bottles has always been central to my work. They range from functional production pieces to more abstract sculptural one-off objects. These are always made from a blown glass form which is transformed by a process of carving, cutting, polishing and sandblasting. Their concern is no longer with function, but with the relationship between the two forms of the bottle and the stopper. In the *Pebble* series, I am extending this vocabulary to explore the relationship and balance between three or more movable forms.

CH, *Contemporary British Glass*, Crafts Council, London, 1993, p.66

Three Pebbles

Handblown, carved, cut and sandblasted
London, England, 1992
Height 23.2cm
V&A: C.306:1-3-1993
Exhibited, *The Glass Show: Contemporary British Glass*, Crafts Council, London, 1993

Training

1967–71 Cardiff College of Education, B.Ed., Sociology and Teacher training

1975–78 Stourbridge College of Art, West Midlands, BA (Hons) Glass and Metalwork

Professional/international

1978–80 Studio at Royal Brierley Crystal, Stourbridge

1980–85 The Glasshouse, London

1985 Set up Glassworks (London) Limited, with Steven Newell (q.v.) and Simon Moore

1993 *The Glass Show*, London

1997 Set up own company, Catherine Hough Glass

Teaching

1980–present Visiting lecturer to Royal College of Art, London; Edinburgh College of Art; Lancashire University; Buckinghamshire Chilterns University College

Max Jacquard

1964 Born London, England

Critical comment

Jacquard told me of two sides to his work and two ways of working. The first is a breathing of life into empty shells: the forms he has that he describes as 'body cases' resemble wasps' nests or tornado shapes. Life is represented by light which changes colour, from reds to blues, hot to cold – the lights represent changing emotions and states of being... These pieces are sometimes shown in relating family groups. [*The Creators*] The husks appear fragile, hanging delicately face to face with us on a human scale...In recent years he has worked with forms that are suggestive without being determined, allowing an ambiguous interpretation of his work. The work for *Solid Air* involves more figurative hanging objects, concentrating on translating the idea of skin. In previous work, texture is used to show directional movement and macro detail; here he looks at wicker, cloth and brick, and how they might armour our body...Max Jacquard places 'technique in the service of ideas', but he is completely absorbed by both concept and skill. He works in a team and often refers to 'we': his own personal work doesn't have to be by his own hand. Jacquard talks of a rift between being seduced and absorbed by beautiful glass and 'finding my own voice within it'. He is lovingly making this work, absorbed in the craft – but equally concerned with saying something with it and making that clear.

Emma Woffenden, *Solid Air*, Crafts Council, 2002, pp.8–9

Artist's statement

Brick Man was originally conceived as part of an installation for the exhibition, *Solid Air*, at the Crafts Council gallery in March of 2002. Entitled *The Creators*, it was an attempt to describe the sense of isolation, self-protection and perhaps a certain brittle vulnerability felt by the artist and the relationship of identity to the artistic ego. Accompanied by two other figures – *Clothman* and *Wickerman*, this body-form represents a kind of protective shell, lovingly crafted from a series of brick-sized plates that resemble a kind of armour. The fact that it is made of glass is an irony which in some way emphasizes the futility of the exercise. The figure hangs in a position of almost mummified repose. He is in suspended animation and as such seems to be waiting for something. There is an obvious connection with the buried warriors of ancient civilizations such as the Sutton Hoo Ship Burial and the Jade Warriors of China. Jacquard cites various influences including archaeology in the making of this piece. The constructions of insects such as wasp nests and larval pupae are also referenced.

MJ, 2003

Brick Man, one of three figures, **The Creators**
Slumped, cut and sandblasted float glass, bound with galvanized wire
Greensand Barn, (Kent) England, 2002
Height 200cm
V&A: C.127-2003
Exhibited with *Clothman* and *Wickerman* as a group, *The Creators*, in *Solid Air, new work in glass*, Crafts Council, 2002, Contemporary Decorative Arts, Sothebys, London, 2003; *Summer Sculpture*, East Grinstead, Kent, 2003

Training
1982–83 Middlesex Polytechnic, London, foundation course
1983–87 Buckinghamshire College, High Wycombe, BA (Hons), 3-D Design, Ceramics & Glass
1987–88 Artist-in-residence, Buckinghamshire College of Art, High Wycombe

Professional/international
1988–89 Assistant to Anita Omitogun; workshop at Tottenham Green Workshops
1993–96 Warrior Studios, Brixton, London
1996–98 Set up Glassforms, Battersea, London
1998 Founder member of artists' group, New London Glass
2001–present Glassforms, Greensand Barn, Kent

Teaching
1994–98 Main lecturer in kiln-formed glass, Buckinghamshire College, High Wycombe
1999 Visiting lecturer, Wolverhampton University
1999–present Lecturer in cast glass, Surrey Institute of Art & Design; Casting summer school, Daedalian Glass, Poulton-le-Fylde, Lancashire; Greensand Glass, Casting workshops, with Angela Thwaites
2002–present Visiting teacher, Twickenham Adult Education College

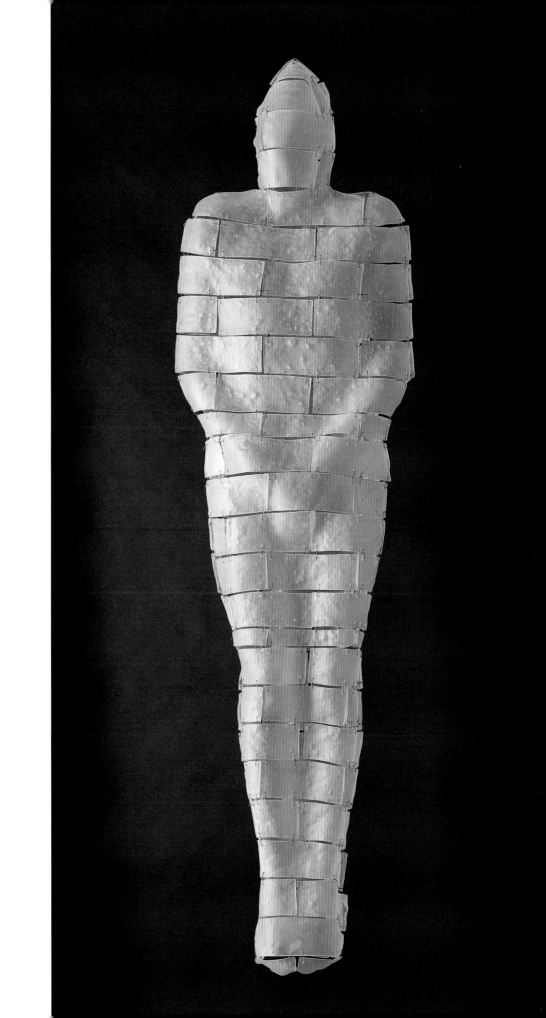

Angela Jarman

1971 Born London, England

Artist's statement

My work has always been influenced by the natural world, and the biological aspects within it. The series that I am making at the moment has evolved through experimentation with ideas relating to feelings invoked in the viewer. I'm trying to create pieces which have a sense of beauty, but which also have a quality about them which makes them slightly strange and disturbing, a lurking sense of unease, something uncomfortably sinister.

AJ, 2003

Evolution 1
Lost-wax cast
London, 2002
Length 45cm
Gift of Paul Bedford
V&A: C.1:1,2-2003
Exhibited, *Angela Jarman*, Crafts Council Gallery, V&A, November, 2002
Illustrated, *Neues Glas/New Glass*, Winter 2003, 4/03, p.28

Training
1993–95 West Surrey College of Art & Design, Farnham, BA (Hons) 3-D Design, Glass

1999–2001 Royal College of Art, London, MA, Glass

Professional/international
1993–95 Assistant to Colin Reid (q.v.), Gloucestershire

1995–2000 Assistant to Tessa Clegg (q.v.) and Diana Hobson (q.v.), London

Teaching
1993–95 Course assistant, Colin Reid

1994 Project tutor, Barnet College of Further Education, HND

2001 Visiting lecturer, Edinburgh College of Art, Glass depatment

Menno Jonker
1968 Born Castricum, The Netherlands

Critical comment
Menno Jonker has established his own set of aesthetic values in which beautiful proportions emphasized by colour elevate the senses. Like many of the Dutch abstract artists he admires, his genre of abstraction is human and very approachable. Its links with nature and with man are clear but subtle. His work can be playful or serious, joyful or contemplative. He has created a modern visual language in glass that builds on tradition and also takes Dutch decorative arts a step further into the 21st century.

Dan Klein, 'Lyrical Abstraction, The Art of Menno Jonker', *Solid Perceptions*, *Menno Jonker*, Amsterdam, 2002

Artist's statement
I have tried to express a feeling of contemplation in *Perception*, a quiet shape with strength, a certain balance. In *Cross* the energy is flowing freely, the movement is bigger, the balance more literal, the solution more sculptural, maybe even more flexible.

MJ, 2003

Cross
Hand-blown, sandblasted, acid-etched and cut
Designed Amsterdam, The Netherlands; made Frome, England, 2001
Gift of the artist
Width 47.5cm
V&A: C.166-2003
Blown by Neil Wilkin and Carl Nordbruch and cut by Steve Frey, under Jonker's direction
Illustrated in *Solid Perceptions, Menno Jonker*, Amsterdam, 2002, p.34
Exhibited, National Glass Museum, Leerdam, The Netherlands, 2002
Photo: Ron Zÿlstra

Training
1984–87 VTA, Art College, Department Individual Arts, Amsterdam
1990–94 Gerrit Rietveld Academy, Theatre Design, Amsterdam
1991 Design classes with Professor Josef Svoboda, Prague, Czech Republic
1992 Hochschule für Angewandte Kunsten (College of Art & Design) Vienna, Austria
1993–97 Classes with A van der Waerden, M de Voogd, E Hermans, Vincent van Ginneke

Professional/international
1997–present Designer, Royal Leerdam Kristal, Leerdam, The Netherlands
1999–2002 Working with Petr Novotny, Lindava, Czech Republic
2000 Working with Davide Salvadore, Murano, Italy
2001 Working with Arie van Loopik, Glascentrum Leerdam, The Netherlands
2001–2002 Designer, Venini, Venice

Teaching
1991 Technische Universiteit, Delft, Art in Architecture
1998– Lecturer at Royal Leerdam Glass, visiting groups programme
2002–03 Art Academy, Maastricht

Other works in the V&A's collection
V&A: C.182:1,2-2003 *Perception*

Alison Kinnaird

1949 Born Edinburgh, Scotland

Artist's statement

…The three parts represent Man, Woman and Child as Past, Present and Future. The Past is represented by Man attempting to free himself from atavistic imagery which, however noble its elements, only suffocates his humanity. His feet are caught in the Web of Time which entangles everyone. The Present is Woman shown as a shell within a shell. This refers to past goddesses whose images are now broken, whose pre-eminence has been dashed and to the rebirth of Woman as a focus of desire whose veiled character, good or bad, has yet to be discovered. It is Woman as flawed Venus, as flawless Virgin, as the Gaelic *Reul na Mara* (Star of the Sea), in whose hands the future is still a mystery. The Future is the Bird Child. The Wren as King of the Birds was killed in Celtic countries in midwinter as a guarantee of fertility for the countryside. The Bird is used here as a symbol of the young soul, bearing the burden of the untouched future…Man is desperately separated from his footprints; Woman, the future as mystery is encircled by, yet separated from, Gaelic but also Botticellian stars engraved on a separate plane; the Child is the only image with which the viewer has inescapable eye contact, but it is the feather-surrounded eye of the murdered wren, bent under the weight of a flawless disc, which is a mirror-like window. *Triptych* explores the iconography of the icon, the symbolism of images of the divine.

AK, 1994

Triptych

Optical glass, wheel-engraved
Gorebridge, Midlothian, Scotland, 1992
Length 36cm
Purchased with help from the National Art Collections Fund
V&A: C.335:1-6-1993
Glass made by Schott, blanks cut to Alison Kinnaird's specification by Kreg Kallenberger
Exhibited, *The Glass Show: Contemporary British Glass*, Crafts Council, 1993

Training

1968–71 Edinburgh University, MA, Celtic Studies & Archaeology

1969 Glass-engraving Workshop, under Harold Gordon

1969–71 Edinburgh College of Art, Engraving, under Helen Monro Turner

2002 Bertil Vallien Masterclass, North Lands Creative Glass, Lybster, Scotland

Professional/international

1975 Set up own workshop, Edinburgh

1978–present Workshop moved to Shillinghill, Midlothian

1993 *The Glass Show*, London

1997 MBE for services to art and music

Teaching

2001 Corning Studio, New York, USA

2002 Frauenau Glass School, Germany

Antoine Leperlier

1953 Born Evreux, France

Critical comment

Antoine Leperlier recalls visiting his grandfather's studio as a small boy and seeing there a skull on an upper shelf. It always held a fascination for him, yet he was cautious about using this always highly charged image in his own work. Only recently does he feel he has reached the necessary maturity to use its unavoidable symbolism with confidence and without slipping into banality.

JHO, conversation with AL, May, 2003

Artist's statement

Le temps est une réalitié resserrée sur l'instant et suspendue entre deux néants

Time is a reality constricted in an instant and suspended between two nothings **(Gaston Bachelard)**

For me, art is a tentative means to catch life. But when you catch it, it dies. This questions the vanity of making art which in turn refers to the vanity of a life which we cannot arrest and make eternal. We are left with memories suggesting eternity, like a lost paradise.

The challenge in *Effets de la Mémoire* was to go further into this tentative state, catching the fleeting instant.

Chaos is the moment just before time is counted. I tried to capture this instant, like a bubble which is about to burst.

The question of this moment is crucial when you consider that we are always 'before' death. Life is as chaos and we find a balance only in the fleeting instant before its loss; this is for me the only acceptable definition of the present. You cannot be at the same time within the present and yet outside it as an artist representing it; but you can show that suspended instant which is between the two, that instant which is neither past nor future. Art tries to show this moment. And glass is the best material with which to do it.

I created a new process to show permanently suspended, this swelling moment between Present and Past, a distortion by an instant of the space between the two.

This process consists of making the hollow form of a skull in a glass cube, which is then held (fused) between sheets of glass. I then fire the work a second time heating it to a point when the air that is confined within the hollow skull begins to expand, like a breath, rising and wanting to escape. I stop the firing at this crucial moment.

With this process I am experimenting in real time with the moment just before the loss, and this is crucial to the work.

There is no other justification of technique in art than to experience the intuition (I do not say concept) or the sensation you wish to represent.

AL, (amended) statement

Effets de la Mémoire XXI 1/1 Chaos
Pâte de verre
Conches, France, 2001
Height 24cm
Gift of Paul Bedford
V&A: C.45-2003
Exhibited, *Antoine Leperlier*, '*L'Instant juste Avant*', Galerie Capazza, Paris/Nançay, 2002

Training
1968–71 Introduced to *pâte de verre* by his grandfather, François Décorchemont

1972–81 Sorbonne, Paris, Philosophy and Fine Arts; Maîtrise et DEA d'Arts Plastiques et de Sciences de l'Art

Professional/international
1981 Lauréat de la Fondation de France

1985 Royal Art Gallery, Osaka, Japan

1989, 1992 Heller Gallery, New York

1992 Habatat Gallery, Farmington Hills, Michigan

1993 Designated Maître d'Art

1996, 2001 Galerie Jean-Claude Chapelotte, Luxembourg

1997 Habatat Gallery, Miami

1998, 2002 Habatat Gallery, Pontiac, Michigan

1998 Miller Gallery, New York

2000 Riley Hawk Galleries, Cleveland, Ohio

2001 Etienne & Rob van den Doel Gallery, The Hague, The Netherlands

Teaching
1988 Canberra School of Art, Australia

1989, 2002 Sars-Poteries, Musée-Atelier du Verre

1997 Pilchuck Glass School, Washington State

2000 Centre des Métiers du Verre

Libenský and Brychtová

Stanislav Libenský, 1921 Born Sezemice. 2002 Died Železný Brod
Jaroslava Brychtová, 1924 Born Železný Brod

Critical comment

Without their industrial base and its attendant state support the Libenskýs' work simply would not exist. Their lives and artistic development have been virtually the reverse of their contemporaries and younger colleagues in the West, where the history of postwar glass art is identified by its conscious escape from and rejection of industry…Libenský's and Brychtová's surefooted route through the vicissitudes of postwar Czech social and political realities – from Prague Spring to Warsaw Pact repression – have brought to the glass stage some of the now most highly regarded works of this period. They have been the prime influence and, in many cases, Libenský was the fondly respected teacher of a whole new generation of Czech glass artists. The present pre-eminence of Czech cast and moulded glass can largely be attributed to them…the Libenskys' are among the few really major figures in modern glass making.

JHO, 'Czech Mates', *Crafts*, Sept./Oct., 1994, pp.42–45

Artists' statement

In 1954 we started working together and created our first collaborative glass piece, *Head-Bowl*, which was based on both a drawing and a sculpted model. Soon, we started to understand the properties of the material. In comparison with other materials, glass is endowed with another dimension – an inner light space – which exists in both clear and transparent colored glass. In clear glass pieces we started to examine the inner optical and light centers and their perceived transformations. We formed colored glass utilizing its properties to achieve a color-light-based sculpture. To this day our creative field is defined by these two concepts. Everything we have done has been achieved through a personal and creative collaboration. Also important has been the fact that we have shared in creating technological conditions for our works. That is vital in the process of development. It is difficult for one person to embrace all the complexities of glass. When terms are created to facilitate technological collaboration, the work is imbued with new impulses, possibilities and strength which furthers development. Every new idea requires practical support. Glass allows us to create a harmony between shapes and penetrating light, and thus to define the essence of light-space and to touch the secrets of this inner space.

SL and JB, Sacral Places, Heller Gallery, New York, 1996

Arcus 1

Mould-melted glass
Probably Pelechov glassworks, 1991
Width 98.5cm
V&A: C.4-1993
The model was made in 1990–91. A number of casts from this model have been made.

Training
Stanislav Libenský

1937–39 Glass schools, Nový Bor and Železný Brod

1939–1944 School of Decorative Arts (Applied Painting and Glass Art), Prague, under Professor Jaroslav Holeček

1945–50 Academy of Applied Arts, Prague, under Professor Josef Kaplický

Jaroslava Brychtová

1945–51 Academy of Applied Arts and of Fine Arts, Prague, under Professor Jan Lauda

Professional/international
Libenský

1945–54 Designer, Bor Glass Company

Brychtová

1950–84 Designer, Železný Brod Glass Company

1954–2002 Libenský and Brychtová working in partnership:

1958 Grand Prix, World's Fair, Brussels

1967 Expo '67 Montreal

1977 Coburg Glass prize, honorary award

1984 Rakow Award for Excellence in the Art of Glass, Corning Museum of Glass, New York State

1993 Retrospective exhibition, Corning Museum of Glass, Corning, USA

Teaching
Libenský:

1963–87 Professor, Glass studio, Academy of Decorative Arts, Prague

Innumerable teaching workshops and lectures in partnership

Other works in the V&A's collection
V&A: C.104-1984 vase, *Orient* or *1001 Nights;* V&A: C.105-1984 vase;
V&A: C.19:1,2-1996 *Winged Head I*

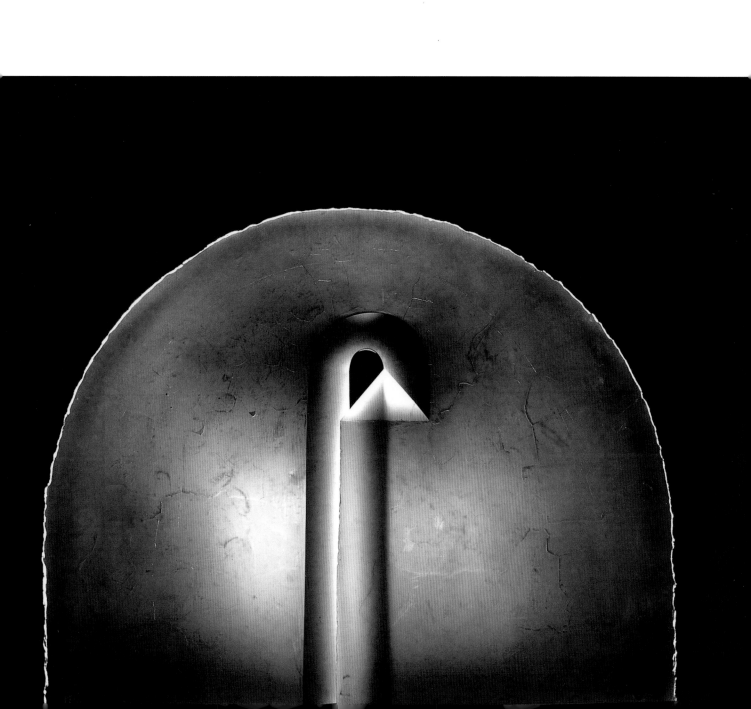

Liz Lowe

1956 Born Leicester, England

Artist's statement

My work echoes experiences and observations of life. Mythologies and ancient civilizations direct my thoughts. The glass is blown into soft sand moulds. Images are applied to the surface by hand painting lustres and enamels or cutting into the glass by sandblasting or engraving.

LL, *Contemporary British Glass*, Crafts Council, London, 1993, p.69

Future Thoughts

Blown into a soft sand mould, painted enamel and lustre, engraved and sandblasted
Leicester, England, 1993
Height 22.7cm
V&A: C.3-1994

Training

1975–78 Leicester Polytechnic, BA (Hons), 3-D Design, Ceramics

1979–81 Royal College of Art, London, MA, Glass

Professional/international

1983–present Own workshop in Leicester, occasionally collaborating with husband, John Heald Cook

1993 *The Glass Show*, London

Teaching

1990–present Visiting lecturer, North Staffordshire Polytechnic; Leicester Polytechnic; Sunderland Polytechnic

Other works in the V&A's collection

V&A: C.230-1987
V&A: C.261:1-5-1993

Dante Marioni

1964 Born Mill Valley, California, USA

Critical comment

Leaf is a perfect demonstration of Marioni's supreme skill in the Venetian *reticello* technique, with none of the distraction of the luscious colouring which is Marioni's other trademark. A textbook example, it was a prize-winner in a competition to use this ancient process in a modern context. Marioni made a leaf, already a favourite form – elongated, quirky, asymmetrical, sculptural. It is larger than expected, and that too is a Marioni trademark. While his aesthetic is rooted in tradition and technique he is an American, with all that implies of contemporary attention-grabbing culture. This glass is reverential and classic, and at the same time demanding and confident; it holds its own in any setting.

Marioni comes from a family of celebrated artists. His father is Paul Marioni, glass and graphic artist; his uncles are the painter, Joseph Marioni, and the sculptor and conceptual artist, Tom Marioni. As a boy he was surrounded by glass-making of the highest quality. Lino Tagliapietra was a family friend, also Richard Marquis, Fritz Dreisbach, Dale Chihuly, and Benjamin Moore. Family summers were spent at Pilchuck. Glass-making is in his bloodstream. Naturally drawn to minimal classicism and rebelling against the prevailing fashion for 'dip and drip' (his words), early on he made goblets, thousands of them, until he was pitch perfect.

JHO

'Lino Tagliapietra once told me that if I made goblets for seven years, I could make anything. Goblets are about figuring things out, working through form, and through the repetition, developing skill'.

'...*reticello*, a net glass technique with air bubbles – a super-fussy, very exacting Italian technique.'

'I like the leaf form. I like the way it's done in 1950s wallpaper or those kitschy 1950s ceramic dishes, and I have always admired the leaf bowls and plates Tyra Lundgren made for Venini. The Leaf Vases are the most unusual form I've made. They have historical references like my other work, but they don't really refer to anything other than a leaf. There's no direct reference to nature in anything else I've made.'

Dante Marioni, quoted in Tina Oldknow, *Dante Marioni Blown Glass*, Hudson Hills Press, New York, 2000, p.50

Reticello Leaf

Hand-blown, *reticello* technique
Seattle, 2001
Height 68cm
Gift of the artist
V&A: C.156-2003
The Queen Margarethe and Prince Henrik's Foundation Prize in *Reticello* 2002, a competition organized jointly by Ebeltoft Glasmuseum and Rosenborg Castle, Denmark. Awarded 1st place, in Category II: 'to make use of the *reticello* technique in a modern context'.
Exhibited, *Reticello 2002*, Ebeltoft Glasmuseum, Denmark

Training
1979 Pilchuck Glass School, Washington State

1982 The Glass Eye Studio, Seattle, Washington State

1983 Penland School of Crafts, Penland, North Carolina

Professional/international
1990 Studio 5 Seibu, Tokyo, Japan

1993 Gallery Nikki, Tokyo

1994 Gallery Nakama, Tokyo

1997 Marina Barovier Gallery, Venice; Contemporary Art Niki, Tokyo; Outstanding Achievement in Glass, Urban Glass Award, New York

2002 Sandra Ainsley Gallery, Toronto, Canada; Queen Margarethe and Prince Henrik Foundation Prize, Denmark

Teaching
1985 Pratt Fine Arts Center (Advanced Glass-blowing)

1987 Canberra School of Art, Australia

1988 Penland School of Crafts

1989–92 Nijima Glass Art Centre, Nijima, Japan

1990–2003 Pilchuck Glass School, Washington State

1991–2004 Innumerable workshops and lectures given internationally

Richard Marquis

1945 Born Bumblebee, Arizona, USA

Critical comment

The *Marquiscarpas* flaunt Marquis's expert knowledge and handling of the *murrine* technique and his unique and inventive response to the history of glass-making and glass design. 'The [*Marquiscarpas*] … are the result of my wonder and admiration of…[ancient] Roman work and Carlo Scarpa's designs for Venini before World War II. I made [the *Marquiscarpas*] …because I pay attention to history. I made them because I wanted to see how I would make them. I made them because to me it was the obvious thing to do.' The form of the *Marquiscarpas* … refers to historic … chalices, ancient Egyptian and traditional African and Asian headrests, and ancient Greek ceramic footed drinking cups …Sometimes Marquis will include a tiny signature *murrina* or another of his typical images, such as a dollar sign or a teapot. In concept and technique, the *Marquiscarpas* are a major accomplishment for the artist and make an equally powerful impression on people familiar with glass as well as those who are not.

Tina Oldknow, Richard Marquis, 'Objects', University of Washington Press, Seattle, 1997, pp.35-6

Artist's statement

The Whole Elk Theory states that if you kill an elk you must use the whole thing – meat, skin, hooves, tail, and so on. These pieces use the leftover end bits of the twisted zanfirico canes that I make and incorporate in other aspects of my work.

RM, Richard Marquis, catalogue, Maurine Littleton Gallery, April 2003

Marquiscarpa (Whole Elk)

Fused, slumped, blown glass and wheel-carved *murrine* technique
Langley, USA, 2003
Width 51.5cm
Gift of Johanna Nitzke Marquis and Caterina Tognon in honour of Ludovico Diaz de Santillana
V&A: C.4-2004
Exhibited, SOFA by Caterina Tognon Arte Contemporanea, New York, 2003

Training
1963–72 University of California, Berkeley, USA, BA Decorative Arts, MA Design

Professional/international
1969–70 Guest designer and Fulbright Scholar, Venini & Co, Venice

1974 Realities Gallery, Melbourne, Australia; touring consultant and lecturer, Craft Council of Australia

1976 Tasmanian Art Museum, Hobart, Tasmania; Queen Victoria Museum, Launceton, Tasmania

1977 Gallery Morronier, Kyoto, Japan

1983, 1989 Auckland Art Museum and Dowse Art Museum, New Zealand

1990, 2003 Sandra Ainsley Art Forms, Toronto, Canada

1993 Gallery Nakama, Tokyo

1998 Caffè Florian, Venice; visiting artist, Waterford Crystal, Ireland

2000 Galerie Rob van den Doel, solo exhibition, The Hague, Netherlands

2002 Ebeltoft Glass Museum, Denmark

Teaching
1970–1 Instructor, University of Washington, Seattle

1972–3 Instructor, San Francisco State University

1976 Artist-in-Residence, Tasmanian College of Advanced Education, School of Art, Hobart, Tasmania

1977–83 Assistant Professor of Art, University College of Los Angeles

Also teaching and workshops internationally

Gayle Matthias

1964 Born Stoke-on-Trent, England

Artist's statement

'A list seemed to express my thoughts in a more direct and simplified form

layers

fragile shells

built-up walls

living through these times

body vessels

clear glass

textural forms

outer shell and inner core'

GM, from *British Studio Glass*, Studio Glass Gallery, London, 1996, p.18

Body 1 (from a series)

Pâte de verre, part-polished, and mirrored glass

London, 1996

Height 25.5 cm

Gift of the artist

V&A: C.183:1-3-2003

Others from this series exhibited in B*ritish Studio Glass*, Studio Glass Gallery, London, Bratislava and Prague, 1996

Training

1983–84 North Staffordshire Polytechnic, Art Foundation

1987 Stourbridge College of Art, BA Hons, 3-D Design, Glass

2002 City & Guilds, Further & Adult Education Teachers' Certificate; Westminster College, Professional Development Certificate, lampworking

Professional/international

1988–90 Assistant to Colin Reid (q.v.)

1990 Assistant to Peter Layton, London Glassblowing Workshop

1991 Assistant to Diana Hobson (q.v.), Pilchuck Glass School, Washington State; artist-in-residence, Bullseye Glass Company, Seattle

1993 Glas Galerie Borgward, Bremen, Germany; *The Glass Show*, London

1994 Artist-in-residence, Les Verriades, Ecomusée, Trelon, France

1995 Artist-in-residence, Platform Verrerie, Vannes le Chatel, France

1996 Artist-in-residence, Cristalleries et Verreries d'Art de Vianne, France; Galeries et Musée, Vianne

Teaching

1993–2003 Westminster Adult Education Centre, London

1997–2001 Visiting lecturer, Barnet College, Wolverhampton University and Central St Martin's, London

2003–present Part-time senior lecturer in Glass, Falmouth School of Art, Contemporary Craft Course, Cornwall

Richard Craig Meitner

1949 Born Philadelphia, USA

Critical comment

You know Richard. Nothing's easy. His work is so evidently purposeful, yet you can't be sure of its purpose. He makes you think: 'What is he thinking?'. It is that challenge that makes his work always worth looking at.

Paul Marioni, 'About Richard Meitner', *Richard Meitner*, Venice/New York/Paris, 2001, p.26

Artist's statement

Unlike some other pieces I have made, with very disconnected image-associations, I have never really thought about *why* I included the specific objects I did. Maybe *Alice* inspired some kind of reverence in me, which prevented this 'vivisection'. Maybe I am lazy. I don't know. I do know that I have, until recently, somehow found it important *not* to do this. Something gets injured in the process it seems to me. What? Subject of a long conversation.

RCM, 2004

It could well be that we will never succeed to understand anything fully, no matter how simple a thing it seems, by examining it from too close by, or bit by bit, however intently and carefully we are able, no matter how sharp our instruments become. Perhaps what we need to do is the opposite. Not to focus our attention, but to unfocus our attention. Maybe we need to learn something. Something which Don Juan, the Yaqui Indian Sorcerer, who is the main character in the books of Carlos Casteneda, taught. What he said was that we can only ever really 'see' a thing, by not looking directly at it!

RCM, unpublished, talk given to the Glass Art Society conference, Corning, NY, 2001

Alice

Handblown, tooled and lamp-worked borosilicate glass, and mixed media
Amsterdam, 1999
Height 50cm
Anonymous Gift
V&A: C.9:1-6-2004
Exhibited, *Richard Meitner*, Braggiotti Gallery, Amsterdam, 2000–1

Training

1972 University of California, Berkeley, USA, BA Art Practice

1974–75 Rijksakademie voor Beeldende Kunst, Amsterdam; Gerrit Rietveld Academy

Professional/international

1976–present Own glass studio, Amsterdam, with Mieke Groot

1980–95 Designer for Royal Leerdam, The Netherlands; Stoelzle Oberglas, Austria; Guerlain, Paris; Val St Lambert glassworks, Belgium; Salviati glassworks, Venice

1983 Coburg Glass Prize, special prize

1983, 1991, 1993, 2000 Galerie Daniel Sarver, Paris

1989 Gottschalk Betz, Frankfurt

1993 *Venezia Aperto Vetro*, guest of honour

1997 *The Glass Skin*, Japan; Galerie Art du Verre, Luxembourg

1997–98 Musée-Atelier du Verre, artist-in-residence; Sars-Poteries, France; *Venezia Aperto Vetro*, invited artist

2000 Galleria d'Arte & di Vetro, Bergamo, Italy; Barry Friedman Gallery, New York; Ernsting Foundation Museum, Coesfeld-Lette, Germany; A&D Galerie, Antwerp, Belgium

Teaching

1981–2000 Leader (with Mieke Groot), Gerrit Rietveld Academy, glass course

1980–present Numerous workshops and lectures internationally

1996 Became named instructor at Sandberg Institute, graduate study, Amsterdam

Other works in the V&A's collection
C.204-1984 Vase; C.31-1999 *Moby*; C.3-2004 *Sea Dog*

Klaus Moje

1936 Born Hamburg, Germany

Critical comment

Working with a restricted range of forms – the shallow bowl, the flat wall panel or the cylindrical vessel – Klaus Moje draws upon the history of glassmaking to create fields of kaleidoscopic luminescence…Since his arrival in Australia in 1982, he has developed this structural language to incorporate the influence of colour and visual drama of the Australian sky and landscape. His characteristic technique of cutting and composing a mosaic of coloured glass allows him to plan the structure of a work before submitting it to the fusing and polishing processes that create depth and subtly alter his configurations. Close inspection of his glass reveals flashes of unexpected brilliance, graphic tensions and fluidities within the serene formality of his elemental compositions.

Robert Bell, *Material Culture: aspects of contemporary Australian craft and design*, National Gallery of Australia, 2002, p.25

[Klaus Moje's] move to Australia had a profound effect on his imagery …the colour and vastness of the Australian landscape and the intensity of light are unlike anything he had seen in Europe and are reflected in the colourful vessels since his arrival in Australia…Moje says: 'In my early years I used to say that there was 20 percent of the Good Lord in my pieces. Today I would say it is closer to 3 to 5 percent of the Good Lord. There must be space for others now!'

…Moje revels in chromatic splendour and says of his work, 'My principal concern is working with colour and achieving something out of it.'

Dan Klein, *Artists in Glass, Late Twentieth-Century Masters in Glass*, Octopus/Mitchell Beazley, 2001, pp.146–147

Untitled

Glass canes, fused, cut, assembled, kiln-fused and slumped, wheel-cut
Tanja, NSW, 2002
Diameter 54cm
Gift of William & Maxine Block, Linda Boone, Kathy & Ferdinand Hampson, Jeffrey & Cynthia Manocherian and Sophie Pearlstein
V&A: C.14-2003

Training

1952–55 Training as a glass-cutter in family business, Hamburg

1957–59 Staatliche Glasfachschule, Rheinbach and Hadamar, Master's Certificate

Professional/international

1961–80 Studio with Isgard Moje-Wohlmuth (now Isgard Wohlmuth), Hamburg

1981 Foster White Gallery, Seattle; Heller Gallery, New York; Habatat Gallery, Detroit

1982 Moved to Australia; founded glass workshop at Canberra School of Art; set up workshop with Brigitte Enders

1986 Glass Art Gallery, Toronto

1987 Habatat Gallery, Miami-Boca Raton, Florida

1995 Retrospective exhibition, touring galleries in Australia, and Museum für Kunst und Gewerbe, Hamburg; Wustum Museum of Fine Art, Racine, Wisconsin, USA

1996, 1998 *Venezia Aperto Vetro*, guest of honour

1997 Artist-in-residence, Nijima, Japan

1999 Rakow Award, Corning Museum of Glass, New York State

2000 Lifetime Achievement Award, Glass Art Society, USA; artist-in-residence, Pilchuck Glass School, Washington State

2001 Hsin Chu Municipal Glass Museum, Taiwan

2002 Artist-in-residence, Nagoya Arts University, Japan

Teaching

1979–present Various teaching posts internationally

1982–91 Head of glass course, Canberra School of Art, Australian National University

William Morris

1957 Born Carmel, California, USA

Critical comment

[Morris's] technical skills are simply astounding: his ability to make glass look like bone, clay, stoneware, bronze, leather or metal is so accomplished that it might appear effortless...But the significance of William Morris's artistry has never rested in his ability to make glass look like something it isn't; he does not wish to fool the eye so much as he wants to inspire the soul, to touch us in a way that extends beyond our retinas toward a consideration of the deeper implications of our own humanity. It is to that end that Morris has focused his own consideration, his own visual rethinking, on the way earlier civilizations have used certain symbolic forms – animals, vessels, weapons, tools, bones – to comment on their highly complex and ambiguous relationship with nature. He is interested not only in representing animals themselves, but in investigating how certain civilizations over the course of human history have chosen to represent them. Even his stylized and hybridized creatures, like the 'rhyton' stags and horses, echo the fine metal and ceramic work of artists from several millennia ago. In a surprising way, Morris's source material is not nature but culture, and specifically those cultures that sensed within animals a powerfully spiritual resonance.

James Yood, *Animals and the Art of William Morris*, Animal/Artefact, Abbeville, 2000, pp.10–11

Situla was probably a bucket or pail for drawing or carrying water...but was more usually applied to the vessel from which lots were drawn: *sitella*, however, was more commonly used in this signification...

William Smith, *A Dictionary of Greek and Roman Antiqities*, John Murray, London, 1875

Engraved Impala Situla

Free-blown glass, wheel-engraved and tooled
Stanwood, Washington, 2000
Height on stand 56cm
Gift of the Artist
V&A: C.57:1,2-2002
Exhibited, *Bombay Sapphire Blue Room*, London and touring, 2001–2002
Illustrated in James Yood and Tina Oldknow: *William Morris: Animal/Artefact*, Abbeville, 2000, p.68
Illustrated, Corning Museum of Glass: Journal of Glass Studies, vol. 45, 2003, p.228

Training

1973–76 California State University, Chico, BA

1977–78 Central Washington University, Ellensburg, Washington State, MA (ceramics)

1978 Pilchuck Glass School, Washington State (driver, assistant to glass-masters, glass-master)

1980 Orrefors Glass School, Sweden

Professional/international

1981 Galerie der Kunsthandwerker, Hamburg; Galerie Fischer, Augsburg, Germany

1981, 1983, 1988 Glass Art Gallery, Toronto

2003 Ebeltoft Glass Museum, Denmark

Teaching

1979–present Pilchuck Glass School, Washington State

1984 Rhode Island School of Design

1985 New York Experimental Glass Workshop; Haystack Mountain School of Crafts, Deer Isle, Maine

1986 New Zealand Glass Society, workshop

1986–1993 Various teaching assignments in the USA

1992, 1994 Nijima Art Glass Centre, Tokyo

Other works in the V&A's collection

V&A: C.55-1981 Vase

Keiko Mukaïde

1954 Born Tokyo, Japan

Critical comment

'I want natural glass like magma,' she says. 'Glass is so beautiful if you don't touch it so much.' Natural is a slippery word and she uses it constantly. The 'naturalness' of glass for her is about mutability, the flow from one soft state to another hard one, and about fragility. In this she discerns a particularly Japanese approach to material culture, an enjoyment of metamorphosis that she finds most particularly in Japanese rock gardens. In these powerful, formal constructs of rock, moss and water, the gardener withdraws at a certain point, and the garden is finished by erosion and the seasons. Mukaide says that in her use of sandcasting, where she kiln-fires sheet glass and networks of glass strands placed in sand-moulds, there is a similar 'withdrawal: I want to be a witness.'

Edmund de Waal, *Essential Elements*, *Crafts*, **July–August, 1995, p.32**

Keiko Mukaïde's bowl was made by trailing spaghetti-sized glass threads into a mould. The technique is simple, but it creates an extraordinary effect. The piece looks rather dangerous as it glistens in the display case. It just about retains a notion of functional form, but the wavy rim explodes with a mass of threads that imply a continuing organic growth. Here the visual dynamic of light playing through clear glass paradoxically creates a tactile invasion of space. It is not a piece one wants to touch.

Janet Barnes (Director of the Crafts Council), *Object of Desire*, **V&A Magazine, Jan–April, 2001, p.11**

Hexagon Wavy Bowl

Glass trailed into a mould, fused
Edinburgh, 1995
Length 47.5cm
Purchased by the Alastair Pilkington Fund
V&A: C.19-1995
Exhibited, *Hot Glass – Cold Glass*,
Contemporary Applied Arts, 1995

Training

1981 Musashino Art University, Tokyo, BA (Hons) Visual Communication Design

1982 Pilchuck Glass School, Washington State, hot glass course

1983 Penland School of Crafts, USA, hot glass course

1987 Pilchuck Glass School, kiln-work course, (with Diana Hobson)

1989–91 Royal College of Art, London, MA, Glass

1995 Sars-Poteries, France, kiln-work (with Warren Langley)

1994 Bild-Werk Frauenau, Germany, with Ursula Huth, S Peretti, J Prince

Professional/international

1992–93 Artist-in-residence, Westminster Adult Education Institute

1993 *The Glass Show*, London

1993–96 Artist-in-residence, Edinburgh College of Art

1995 Artist-in-Residence, Sars-Poteries, France

1995 Sars-Poteries Musée-Atelier

1996 Galerie L, Hamburg; *Venezia Aperto Vetro*, invited artist

1997 Braggiotti Gallery, Amsterdam, The Netherlands

2003 Ebeltoft Glass Museum, *Spirit of Place*, Denmark

Teaching

2000-present Part-time research fellow in Glass, Edinburgh College of Art

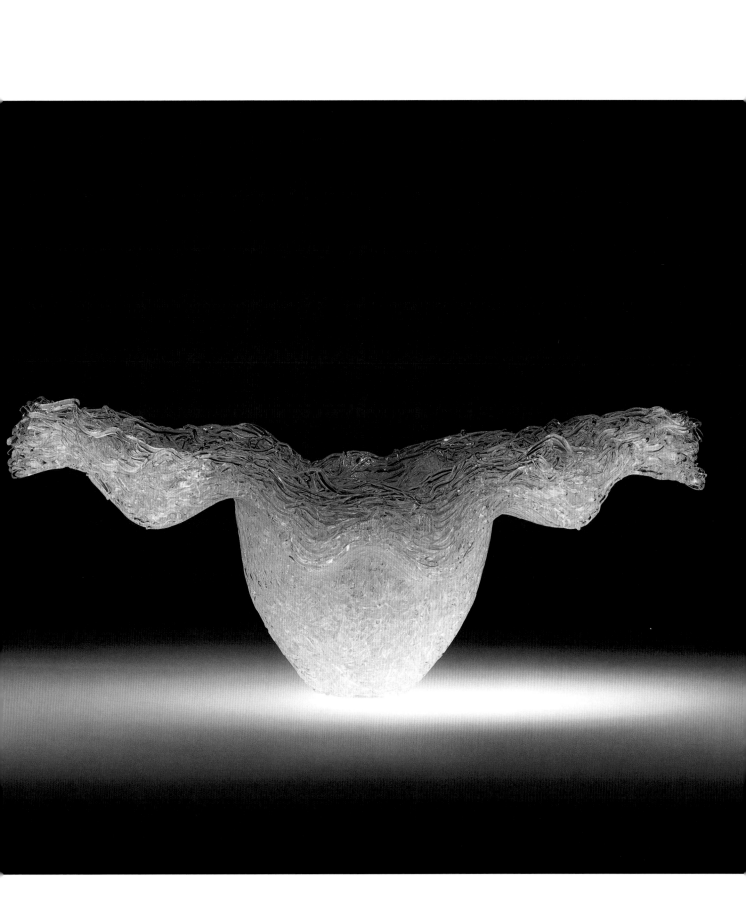

Steven Newell

1948 Born Springfield, Massachusetts, USA

Critical comment

Steven Newell's work doesn't need elaborate variety of form, or dazzling combinations of colour, because it relies on imagery; the mysterious picture is the main point, and the questions it raises, and we are not to be distracted from it. Further questions are often asked by the titles. Narrative, sometimes autobiographical, these scenes and encounters of mythical or prosaic figures, people and creatures and amalgamations, simply need a quiet, spacious, warm object on which to live…The sand-blaster is the surprising means to such subtlety. Difficulty is perhaps the great facilitator after all – masking out the drawing inside a deep concave shape, achieving fine degrees of shading with fairly random spatterings of sand – these conditions make for the intensity of an image compromised with a material, that he would not achieve on paper.

Alison Britton, *Glassworks (London) Limited,* **Contemporary Applied Arts, London, 1989**

What are the sources of his individualistic iconography? Newell's subject-matter ranges from the Old Testament to love and birth in the land of the modern bedsitter. His subjects may be saints or saxophonists, senators or surfers. His eye roves over the human condition in a spirit of amused compassion; humour is central to many of his themes. What we see is not art for art's sake nor crafts for craft's own purposes. It is instead a joyous, freewheeling amalgam of the limitless possibilities of form, colour, decoration and symbolism when harnessed to a singular vision…

Giles Auty, *Steven Newell,* **Contemporary Applied Arts, London, 1994**

Plaque, Adam and Eve

Hand-blown, sandblasted
Diameter 56cm
V&A: C.153-1991
Exhibited, *Colin Reid*, Crafts Council Gallery, V&A, 1991

Training

1968–69 Kansas City Art Institute, USA, Ceramics and Glass

1969–72 Carnegie-Mellon University, Pittsburgh, USA (Ceramics and Glass)

1972–74 Royal College of Art, London, MA, Glass

Professional/international

1974 Founder-member (director), The Glasshouse, Covent Garden, London

1977 Coburg Glass Prize, most promising newcomer award, Germany

1983, 1984, 1987, 1998 Miharudo Gallery, Tokyo

1985 Set up Glassworks (London) Ltd with Catherine Hough (q.v.)

1987 La Galleria, Frankfurt-am-Main, Germany

1990 Galerie Majault, Paris

1993 *The Glass Show*, London; Tokyo Museum of Arts & Crafts, Japan

1995 Blås & Knada, Stockholm, Sweden

1998 Retrospective exhibition, Nitsu Gallery, Japan; *Venezia Aperto Vetro*, invited artist

1999 Set up Artfull glass studio

2001 Tokyo department store

Other works in the V&A's collection

V&A: C.22-1980 *Aquatic plate*
V&A: C.23-1980 *Brown man bowl*
V&A: C.99-1981 *Two profile bowl*
V&A: C.229-1987 *Jug*
V&A: C.144-1993 *Jug* (with Carol McNicholl)
V&A: C.82-1994 *Fish vase*

Kerttu Nurminen

1943 Born Lahti, Finland

Critical comment

Kerttu Nurminen began her career at Nuutajärvi glassworks, now part of Iittala Glass, in 1973. She has been one of the mainstays of the serial production there for over 25 years and is the designer of some of their most successful, long-running standard lines: the *Mondo* range of drinking glasses and decanters is the best known. This year [1997] Nurminen was awarded the prestigious Kaj Franck Design Prize, presented annually to a designer or team actively involved in crafts and industrial design to high aesthetic, ecological, technical and ethical standards. In recent years she has taken up the Swedish Graal technique and has produced an immensely strong series of vases and goblets, opulent in design and substantially proportioned as here in *Kartano*. The Finnish title refers specifically to the immediate locality – the village, glassworks and estate of Nuutajärvi. Given the name *On Farmer's Land* in English, this work, like much Finnish art and design, draws for inspiration on the landscape and often harsh climate of the country.

JHO, unpublished, for the exhibition *New Finnish Glass*, V&A, 1997

Vase, Kartano (On Farmer's Land)
Graal technique, with painting in lustre
Nuutajärvi glassworks, iittala oy ab, Finland, 1995
Height 34.5cm
Gift of Hackman Designor AB
V&A: C.177-1997
The glass blown by Eelis Kankainen; engraved and painted by Kerttu Nurminen
Exhibited, *Finnish Postwar Glass*, Vardy Gallery, Sunderland University, 1996; *New Finnish Glass*, V&A, 1997
Illustrated, Jack Dawson, *Finnish Postwar Glass*, University of Sunderland, 1996, pl.56

Training
1962 Business college

1966–70 Institute of Industrial Arts, Helsinki, Ceramics

Professional/international
1972–present Designer and artist, Nuutajärvi glassworks, (iittala oy ab, Hackman Designor since 1991)

1977 Coburg Glass Prize, honorary award, Germany

1987– Graphic design for Hackman Designor and freelance

1992 Stockholm Art Museum, Sweden

1996 Kaj Franck Design Prize

1998 *Venezia Aperto Vetro*, invited artist; Galeria San Niccoló, Venice

Other works in the V&A's collection
Glass designed for iittala-Nuutajärvi production

Yoichi Ohira

1946 Born Tokyo, Japan

Critical comment

The last collection of one-of-a-kind pieces, *Pastel* and *Glass Paste* are based on the brilliant colours of opaque *tesserae*. These are sometimes shiny on the surfaces, and sometimes rendered matt by cold finishing. The glass quality is heightened by the large and small 'window' compositions of transparent glass in these pieces. Brilliant multicoloured glass is alternated with subtler colors rarely used in glass (such as brown, mustard yellow and black) and, unexpectedly, with rare pure monochrome work similar to alabaster. The smaller dimensions, the painstaking attention to details occasionally of symbolic value, the delicate weaving of the rods and the tesserae visible in the monochrome surfaces as well, sharply contrast the exaggeration of works by other contemporary glass artists.

Rosa Barovier Mentasti, 'Yoichi Ohira', in *New Traditions in Glass from Venice*, Barry Friedman Gallery, New York, 1998, p.40

'The technique that I have used in recent years can be described as mosaic composition with glass canes and the use of glass powders,' explains Ohira. 'This allows me to draw a parallel with the world of high fashion. I personally prepare the fabrics (in glass), these are then sewn and shaped (blown and cut) into costumes (works in glass) by the tailors (the glass-masters).'...Despite his decades-long residence in Venice, Ohira's style is also inseparable from his heritage. The shapes, opacity of color, finishes and textures are closely tied to Japanese ceramics, lacquer, and bamboo objects, as well as textile design...One palm-sized cup looks as if it were carved from Persian turquoise; the blue-green is barely translucent and sufficiently cool to suggest that it is glass. What makes the piece spring to life is a tiny tranparent red-framed 'window': as that mouse-sized view punctures the vessel wall, it conjures memories of universal blue worlds.

Susanne K Frantz, *Yoichi Ohira's better beauty*, Neues Glas/New Glass, no.90, Spring, 2003, p.22–27

Vaso a mosaico (mosaic vase)
from the collection Pasta Vitrea
(glass paste)
Fused canes, hand-blown
Venice (Murano), Italy; 1998
Height 19.5cm (C.1) or 20cm (C.2)
Gift of the artist
V&A: C.1 to 2-1999
Hand-blown by Livio Serena

Training
1969 Graduated from Kuwusawa Design School, Tokyo

1970–71 Glass-blowing apprenticeship, at Kagami Crystal, Tokyo

1971 Glass-blower, glassworks, Chiba province

1973–78 Accademia di belli Arti (Academy of Fine Arts), Venice; Sculpture and Aesthetics of Glass (degree dissertation), under Alberto Viani

Professional/international
1973 Began collaboration with Egidio dio Constantini's La Fucina degli Angeli glass studio, Venice

1978– Independent artist in metal and glass

1987–90 Designer for, then artistic director of Vetreria de Majo

1992 Established own independent studio in Venice

1993 Began collaboration with glass-master Livio Serena

1996, 1998 *Venezia Aperto Vetro*, invited guest

2000 Galerie Michel Giraud, Paris

2001 Rakow Commission 2001 award, Corning Museum of Glass, NY

2000, 2001, 2002 Barry Friedman Gallery, New York

Other works in the V&A's collection
V&A: C.2-1999
See the drawings for these in the collections of Word & Image Department, E.185,186-2000

Heikki Orvola

1943 Born Helsinki, Finland

Critical comment

This work, with its companion, *Minotaurus*, is a unique piece from a group of twenty such works made in 1994. In designing these, Orvola was deeply influenced by an exhibition of the work of the Paris-based Russian Suprematist artist, Ivan Puni (Jean Pougny), but these simple, architectonic shapes are also typical of Orvola's designs for textile and ceramic decoration. Here, three-dimensionally, the flat geometry assumes a post-modern character.

JHO, unpublished, for the exhibition *New Finnish Glass*, V&A, 1997

The precise finishes and laborious detail of the sculptures are typical of Orvola. Despite the lively shapes, the overall impression is one of balance. The works are given a sense of stability by the finely balanced coloured surfaces. The clear basic colour is combined with reflecting mirror surfaces and the coolness of matt glass. Almost all the surfaces of the sculptures composed of several elements are ground. The character of the pieces is far from the carefree inexactitude of the glass-blowing workshop.

Press release, Hackman Designor, 1994

Stardust

Mould-blown glass, cut and assembled
Nuutajärvi glassworks, iittala oy ab, Finland, 1994
Height 30cm
Gift of Hackman Designor
V&A: C.109-1996
The glass blown by the Nuutajärvi glass team, cut by Seppo Laasko, assembled by Heikki Orvola
Exhibited, *Finnish Postwar Glass*, Vardy Gallery, Sunderland University, 1996; *New Finnish Glass*, V&A, 1997

Training

1963–68 Institute of Industrial Arts, Helsinki, Ceramics

1976 Pilchuck Glass School, Washington State

Professional/international

1968–83 Designer, Nuutajärvi glassworks

1970–present Embroiderer

1976–84 Freelance designer, Järvenpää Enamel

1983– Freelance designer, glass

1984 Galerie Inart, Amsterdam

1985–95 Freelance designer, Marimekko textiles

1992 Freelance design, Alessi, Italy

1994 Italcris Gallery, Madrid

1994–present Freelance designer, Arabia and Rörstrand

1996, 1998 *Venezia Aperto Vetro*, invited artist

1999– Freelance designer, SC Sarner Cristal AG, Switzerland

2001 Freelance design, Iwate Industrial research Institute, Morioka, Japan

2002 Co-operation project, Encuentros, Mexico

Teaching

1968–91 Assistant teacher, University of Art & Design, Helsinki, Ceramics and Glass

Other works in the V&A's collection

V&A: C.44&A-1988 *Pyramidi*
V&A: C.110-1996 *Minotaurus*

Zora Palová

1947 Born Bratislava, Czechoslovakia (now Slovakia)

Critical comment

In this work Zora Palová demonstrates a wealth of experience and a deep understanding of the behaviour of light within cast glass. She comes from a generation of students of the Czech master, Václac Cigler, whose great contribution has been to instil this understanding in his students. Beyond that, Palova has developed a personal language that refers to bridges and connections. She takes special pleasure in discovering and responding to the shared heritage of Celtic forms and decoration which stretches from her native Slovakia to the north of England where she has now spent more than eight years. In *Daisy Seed* she uses balance and tension, strength and fragility, qualities which have a particular resonance in cast glass. Choosing a vibrant acid yellow, using partly uranium-coloured glass, she has defined a simple, almost primitive form and then boldly intersected it. Within the space created, light bounces from intersected wall to intersected wall. Adding even further to the sculpture's animation, the internal bubbling and crustiness, a result of the casting process, are welcomed for their unpredictable beauty. Far from being a dormant seed, this form springs into life. Its innocent title belies its conceptual and physical strength.

JHO, 2003

Daisy Seed

Cast glass, partly ground, sandblasted and acid-polished
Bratislava, Slovakia, 2000 (the original model made in Sunderland)
Length 59cm
Gift of Juliette Boisseau and David Hardman
V&A: C.46-2003
Exhibited, *Zora Palová*, Pokorna Gallery, Prague, 2002 and Pokorna Gallery, SOFA, New York, 2002

Training

1963–67 High School of Applied Arts, Bratislava, Woodcarving (under Professor L Korkos)

1969–71 Academy of Fine Arts, Bratislava, Painting (under Professor L Cemicky)

1971–75 Academy of Fine Arts, Bratislava, Glass in Architecture (under Professor Václav Cigler)

Professional/international

1975–96, 2003 Freelance artist in Bratislava, working with Stepan Pala

1991 Art & Glass Gallery A Schmalreck, Munich

1996 Sculpture commission, *Guardian*, Association of Dutch Insurers, The Hague, The Netherlands

1997 Galerie du Verre, Luxembourg

1998 Sculpture commission (with Stepan Pala), National Glass Centre, Sunderland, England

1999 Habatat Galleries, Florida; sculpture commission, Sculpture Park, Goodwood, England

2000 Jean-Claude Chapelotte Gallery, Luxembourg; Koganezaki Glass Museum, honourable mention, Japan

Teaching

Lecturer, School of Arts, Nitra, Slovakia

1988–1998 Various symposia in Czechoslovakia, Czech Republic and Slovakia

1996–present Research Professor, now Visiting Professor, University of Sunderland, England

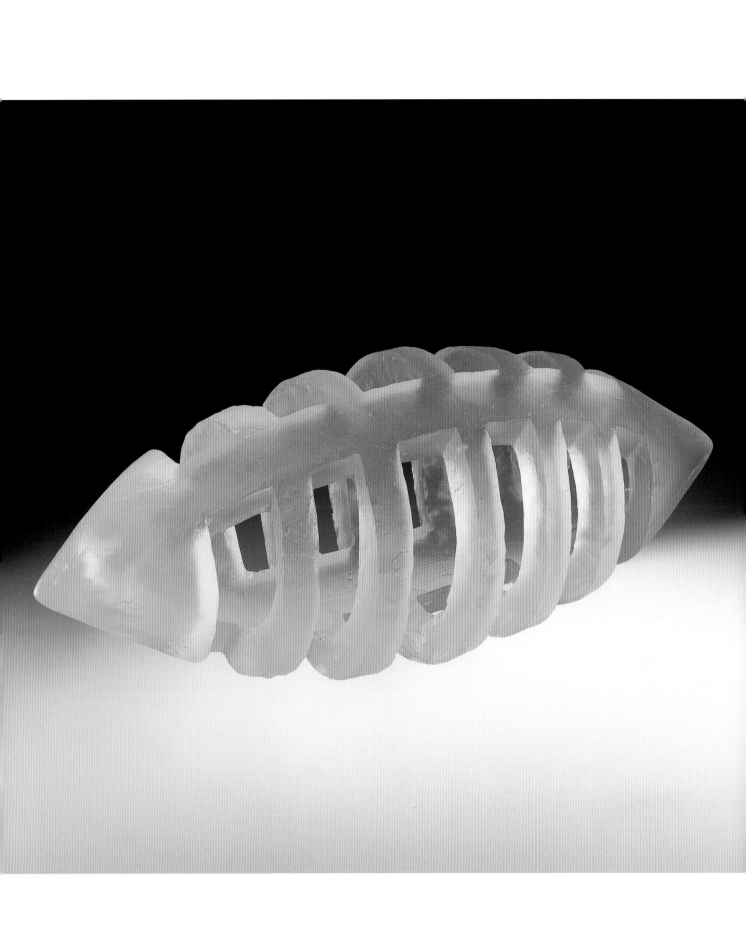

Danny Perkins

1955 Born Frankfurt, Germany (American)

Critical comment

Danny Perkins creates elongated objects that float color fields and undulate them in space. Most commonly they would be described as painted, blown glass vessels. Slim at the base, their precariously towering bodies open outwards towards the top to create sheer volume. Each of the forms is cracked and broken. Then, each shard is colored with oil paint and finally the entire object is reconstructed.

Perkins describes his process as an emotionally reactive one. He is responding to the fragments of glass and paint. In an intensely personal statement he adds, 'My creative process is an intuitive journey that takes me to levels beyond what I intellectually know. I feel honesty and humility at the time of creation, echoing one of the basic creative concepts defined by Kandinsky as "inner need".'

Katja Garrow, Heller Gallery, New York, 1991

Artist's statement

I am a student of the Abstract Expressionists. Creating sculpture makes the connection between my psyche and body. First, it is a physical and group effort to blow and form my large fluid forms; then a solitary and intimate process of breaking them. The colors, with the forms I use, are emotions; they are love, sex, god, pain and joy. I have developed relationships with the colors over the years: when I paint the shards the colors have faces that I know intimately. [Painting]…is combining different emotions in varying weights. Reassembling the pieces has all that mixture of feelings in one. One has joy, another is pain: as a group they sing. My work is about the deep richness of experiencing life; of going 100 miles per hour with your eyes closed crying and laughing at the same time.

DP, 2003

Yellow on Purple
Slumped, fractured, assembled, sandblasted, painted
Seattle, USA, 1991
Height 137cm
Pledged Gift of Dale & Doug Anderson through the American Friends of the V&A Museum Inc. and on loan to the V&A Museum
Exhibited, Heller Gallery, New York, 1991

Training
1976– No formal training

1976–79 Craft Farm, teaching assistant in hot glass workshop, stained glass production

1979 Studying under Henry Suma, hot glass

1985 Student under Lino Tagliapietra (q.v.), Pilchuck Glass School, Washington State

Professional/international
1981–82 Urrere/Perkins studio: glass production

1982–83 John Lewis Glass

1987 Artist-in-residence, Pilchuck Glass School

2000 Pilchuck Glass School, artist assistant to Jim Dine

Teaching
1984 Pilchuck Glass School, teaching assistant to Dan Dailey

1986 Pilchuck Glass School, teaching assistant to Paul Marioni

2001 Instructor, Pilchuck Glass School

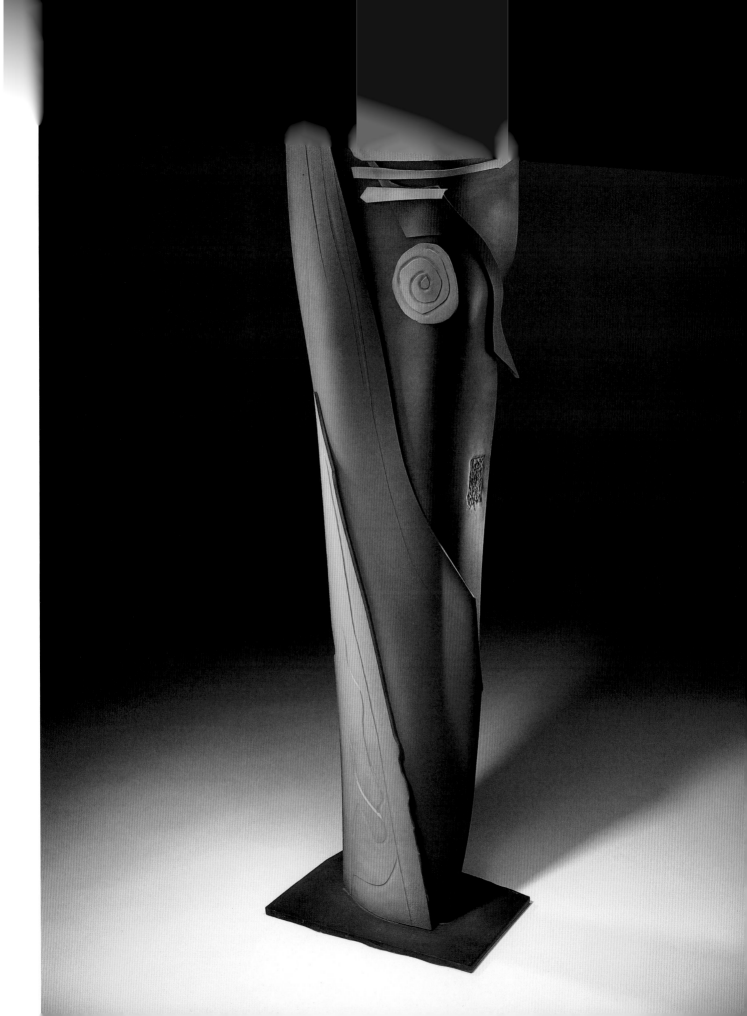

Kirstie Rea

1955 Born Canberra, Australia

Critical comment

In 2002 she spent some months in Lincolnshire, England. For the first time she saw the regular, furrowed marks of machinery – the plough – which are such an integral part of the English landscape. Indeed, here in England the idea of 'countryside' traditionally conjures up images of autumnal, bare ploughed fields. Rea had rapidly to develop a new vocabulary to describe what was, for her, a very different environment. *Touch* is a gentle, rhythmic evocation of the flat Lincolnshire landscape: a landscape described by these man-made lines and over a year inexorably absorbed – but never completely vanquished by the changing seasons.

JHO, 2003

Artist's statement

Rhythmic flows in time and touch, connection to country and place.

KR, 2004

Kirstie Rea has said that her work 'focuses on both natural and imposed elements within the Australian landscape, drawn together by the power and strength of the environment, time and their enduring co-existence. These works are an expression of the reconciliation between the natural and imposed elements resulting in harmony and balance over time.'

KR, *Venezia Aperto Vetro: Essentially Canberra*, Venice, 1998, p.188

Touch

Kiln-formed and wheel-cut
Canberra, Australia, 2002
Height 84 cm
Gift of Bullseye Glass
V&A: C.2:1-3-2004
Exhibited, *Places*, Bullseye Connection
Gallery, Portland, Oregon, USA, 2003

Training

1979–85 Informal stained glass courses and workshops on design, lampworking, neon photo image and painting on glass

1986 Canberra School of Art, BA

1988 International master workshop in glass (kiln-formed techniques), Canberra

1987, 1994 Pilchuck Glass School, Washington State

Professional/international

1987 Established studio in Canberra

1993 Artist-in-residence, Edith Cowan University, Washington, USA

1994 Artist-in-residence, Bullseye Glass Co, Portland, Oregon

1998 *Venezia Aperto Vetro: Essentially Canberra*, invited artist

2000 Bullseye Connection Gallery, Portland, Oregon

2001 Silver Prize, Kanazawa International Glass Exhibition, Japan

2002 English Rural Residency, Lincolnshire, England

Teaching

1987–2001 Part-time lecturer, Canberra Institute of the Arts, glass workshop

1987–2003 Lecturer, glass workshop, Canberra School of Art, Australian National University

1997–98, 2001 Wanganui Polytechnic and Summer School, New Zealand

1999 Quay School, Art Gallery, Wanganui

1999–2003 Teaching posts in USA, Italy, England, Germany, Austria and Scotland

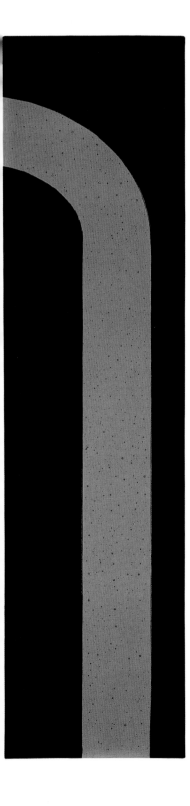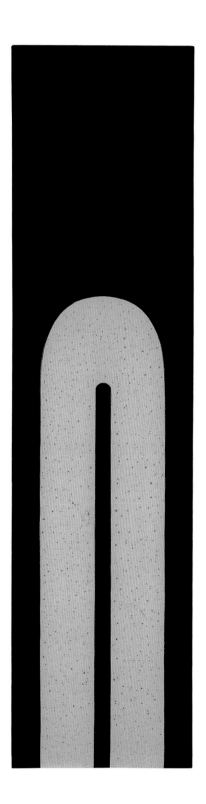

David Reekie

1947 Born Hackney, London, England

Artist's statement

With this eagerness to protect ourselves from the world around us comes the problem of loss of identity as we huddle together for safety. This has made me think more about the individual. As an artist I find it relatively easy to define my individuality. When I am making a piece of work I will model each figure individually and construct a unique sculpture. So making precise moulds to produce clones of a wax figure and then to cast these for *A Captive Audience?* was a refreshing departure from this way of working. I find it visually exciting to be dealing with groups of identical forms and having one which is just slightly different. Working in this way has now allowed me to create crowds of figures with which to explore the subject of identity.

DR, 2000

In his depiction of humdrum situations and our all-too-often indecisive or inadequate responses, Reekie is prepared to chance a degree of risk unmatched by any other maker. He is only interested in exploring ideas; his glass must illuminate these purposefully. Unlike many of his contemporaries, the intrinsic beauty of glass holds little fascination for Reekie; in his world the material must be pressed into the service of narrative and comment. His telling explorations of humankind's obsessions are unique in contemporary British glass and they tread a fine line between comedy and tragedy. His work has often been compared to the biting comment of 18th-century caricaturists. The Hogarthian tradition, with its unblinking observation of common failings, certainly provides a context in which to set Reekie's work, but he himself claims a very wide spread of rather more gentle interests and influences, from the spare, elegant drawings of the Finnish architect, Alvar Aalto, to the Surrealist paintings of René Magritte.

JHO, Introducing 'David Reekie', *David Reekie*, privately published, Norwich, 2001, p.6

A Captive Audience?

Lost-wax cast glass, with wood, metal, cotton
Norwich, England, 2000
Height 74.5cm
Gift of Paul Bedford
V&A: C.112:1-14-2000
Exhibited, *David Reekie Retrospective*, Norwich Castle Museum, 2001

Training

1967–70 Stourbridge College of Art, Glass, Sculpture, under Renie Stevens, Harry Seager and Keith Cummings (q.v.)

1972–73 Birmingham College of Art Education

Professional/international

1975–80 Fellow in Glass, Lincolnshire and Humberside Arts

1975–86 Workshops in Lincoln and Stoke-on-Trent

1986–present Workshop in Norwich

1991, 1993, 1995, 1996 Miller Gallery, New York, USA

1992 Galerie Suzel Berne, Paris

1993 *The Glass Show*, London

1994 International Council Member, Pilchuck Glass School, Washington State

1996 *Venezia Aperto Vetro*, guest of honour

Teaching

1974–75 Halesowen School, Worcestershire

1976–86 Lecturer in Glass at North Staffordshire Polytechnic

1988 Winston Churchill Fellow, Alternative Architectural Glass in USA

1990–91, 93 Visiting lecturer, Pilchuck Glass School

1992 Visiting lecturer, Espace Verre, Montreal, Canada

1993–present Various teaching appointments throughout UK and in New Zealand

Other works in the V&A's collection

V&A: C.257:1,2-1993 *Greek Head V*

Colin Reid

1953 Born Poynton, Cheshire, England

Critical comment

One is immediately impressed by the quiet control and rich language of Colin Reid's work, by his clear-sighted and down-to-earth approach. There is a freshness, epitomized in the clean-cut outline of his yellow cottage, perched high above the Chalford Valley, embracing wind and sky, yet with a sense of self-containment. His studio, a few miles away, is in one of the old stone woollen mills which punctuate the thickly wooded, steep-sided valleys in this part of Gloucestershire. It is well equipped with much of the machinery constructed through his own ingenuity, designed for specific needs.

Texture, movement and flow provide his major areas of exploration, combining energetic elements into a harmonic unity. Bold, well-defined forms, enclosing a wealth of intricate detail, speak for themselves, expressing stillness yet reflecting a state of universal motion. Adjusted perspectives give illusory qualities of depth. Contrasted rough and polished surfaces control light within the form, inducing prismatic colors in addition to those inherent in the metal. Each piece is carefully worked out with plaster or wax models, so that while there is an intuitive use of chance and change during firing, the overall process is carefully orchestrated and controlled.

Stephen Procter, 'Colin Reid – an introduction', *Colin Reid*, Kurland/Summers Gallery, Los Angeles, California, USA, 1984

By taking moulds directly from a variety of natural sources such as tree bark, molehills, fungi and Cotswold stone, he developed a vocabulary of forms and textures with which to 'play', dissecting and reassembling as desired. With a masterly control of formal and organic elements, he explores the natural movement and flow of cast glass in elegant, archetypal shapes. Crosses, triangles and spirals contain beautiful veils of colour and minute bubbles that are trapped as the glass melts and flows into the mould during the kiln-firing, ultimately to be revealed by lengthy and painstaking grinding and polishing.

Peter Layton, *Glass Art*, A&C Black, London, 1996, p.156

Untitled

Lost-wax cast optical glass, cut and polished, with internal veiling; copper patina.
Stroud, England, 1999
Width 53.5cm
Gift of Paul Bedford
V&A: C.10-2000
Exhibited, *Colin Reid*, Crafts Council Gallery, V&A, 1999

Training

1970–72 St Martin's School of Art, London

1975–77 Trained and worked in industry

1978–81 Stourbridge School of Art, BA, 1st Class Hons, Glass, with Professor Keith Cummings (q.v.)

Professional/international

1981–present Own studio in Stroud, Gloucestershire

1985 Coburg Glass Prize, honorary prize, Germany; Westminster Gallery, Boston, MA

1987, 1989, 2000 Maurine Littleton Gallery, Washington, DC

1990 Galerie Gottschalk-Betz, Frankfurt am Main; Galerie L, Hamburg

1990–91 Artist-in-residence, Carrington Polytechnic, Auckland, New Zealand

1992 Galerie L, Hamburg and touring New Zealand

1991, 1993 Miller Gallery, New York; Helander Gallery, Palm Beach, Florida

1993 *The Glass Show*, London

1996 *Venezia Aperto Vetro*, invited guest

2000, 2001 Museo De Arte En Vidrio De Alcorcon, Madrid; Galerie B, Sinzheim, Baden-Baden, Germany

2002 Etienne & Rob van den Doel, The Hague, The Netherlands

Teaching

1999–2002 Visiting professor, University of Wolverhampton

Other works in the V&A's collection

V&A: C.97&A&B-1982 *Untitled Form*
V&A: C.34-1992 *Untitled Form*

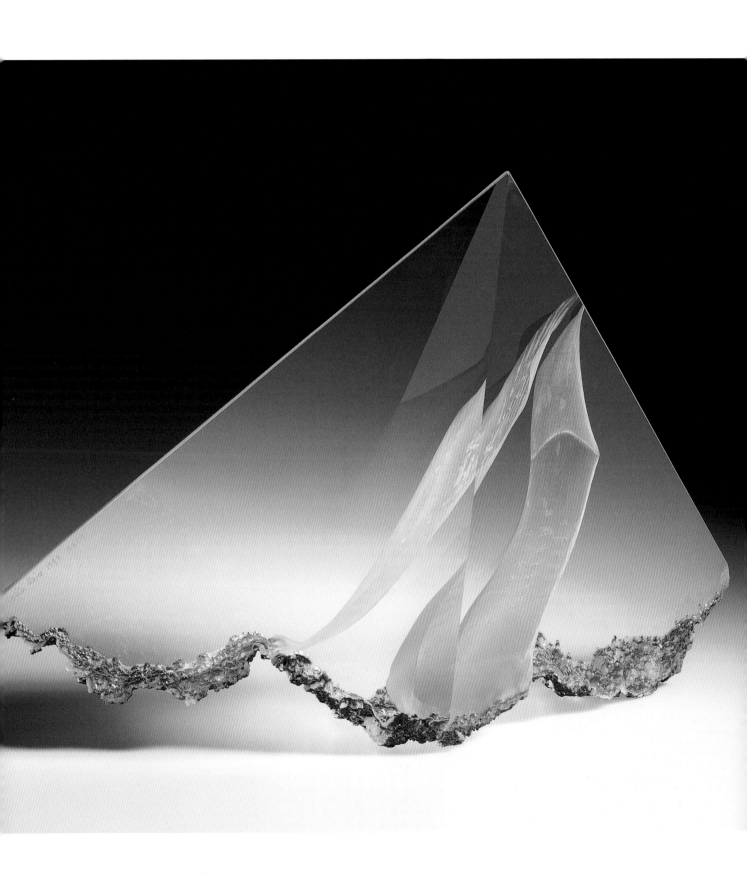

Colin Rennie

1973 Born Los Angeles, USA

Artist's statement

Throughout my life I have been engrossed in the organic…I have found inspiration in the duality between the simple existence of form and aesthetics in nature and the human developmental urge to understand and categorize and dissect and reduce…I want to create forms that are beautiful and deadly, symbolic or obscure, or allusive and defined. Drawing is the basis of my creative process, as I draw I try not to think of meaning, I let the drawings erupt from somewhere and then pick up the pieces and collate the fragments into an assemblage…As the object develops through the process of making, both glass-blowing and cold-working, the form is distilled. One aspect of glass-blowing is that it is either not possible or extremely difficult to create certain forms. The real-ization of an object in glass that has originated in the unconstrained sketchbook is necessarily for myself a process of distillation…Recently I have been experimenting with carving and shaping techniques that involve the removal of large amounts of this extraneous glass and hand-finishing techniques that curve and shape facets, impossible in hot glass alone. This new venture currently is forming the basis of my continuing work both conceptually and physically.

Conjoin is a development from an earlier series…It's the first of its kind in that it revolves around a central joint, the two previous works I made were stand-alone. The strength in Conjoin is that each part relies on the other for stability and, I suppose, included in the subconscious thinking behind the work is an essence of relationship and balance.

CR, 2002

Conjoin

Blown, lathe-cut, hand and machine-polished
National Glass Centre, Sunderland, 2002
Length 48.5cm
Acquired with the assistance of the Alastair Pilkington Fund
V&A: C.47:1,2-2002
Exhibited, 9x9, Glass Art Gallery, London, 2002

Training

1991–95 Edinburgh College of Art, BA, lst Class (Hons), Glass

1995–6 Edinburgh College of Art, M.Des., Glass

Professional/international

1992 Assistant to Adrian McStay, Newport-on-Tay

1996 Artist-in-residence, Edinburgh College of Art, Glass Department

1998, 2003 Clara Scremini Gallery, Paris

2003–present Artist-in-residence, University of Sunderland

Teaching

1999–2001 Senior lecturer in Glass, University of Wolverhampton

Ann Robinson

1944 Born Auckland, New Zealand

Artist's statement

...during this period the strong and recurring identification with the land, its erosive processes (which were mirrored in the glass-making process), and rhythmic patterns associated with plant forms begins to assert its dominance. This is manifested first in the patterns and designs carved onto the individual vessels, developing later to take over the form of the vessel itself. The *Nikau Series* and the later *Cactus Vase* provide clear examples of the plant form with the vessel form. Robinson speaks of the influence of the natural environment when she says: 'When I walk through the bush, I observe the detail; very closely – the criss-cross of the nikau, the way the flax rises up from its base. Something in us responds to the flow of rhythmic patterns. The eye picks out the harmonies, almost like music. I like the idea that my pieces read musically.'

First published in Joanne Wane, Dances of Light, Pacific Way, 1995, p.47 and modified in Ann Robinson Casting Light, A Survey of Glass Castings 1981–97, Dowse Art Museum, Lower Hutt, New Zealand, Laurence Fearnley, 1997

Karekare, a name derived from the Maori word meaning eager, agitated or disturbed, is an apt description of the place where wild seas meet craggy rocks and black sand coastline is surrounded by dense native bush...

The forms and patterns in my work reflect the intensity and extremes experienced in this environment. In turn, the sharp clear quality of light and ever-changing weather patterns affect my perception, understanding and use of colour.

I am by inclination a vessel-maker. The generous forms evoke many layers of meaning and interpretation and offer a rich 'canvas' for expression. For me vessels embody all that has historically transpired, from the earliest mortar, to ritual, religious and ceremonial vessels, even bowls that talk to satellites. They are a means of offering and sharing, of receiving and transmitting and protecting.

Concerned with the timelessness of beauty, my personal 'poetry' has always centred on a deep love and reverence for the natural world. The rhythmic patterns of life and growth translate readily into my work. These patterns, absorbed and interpreted through close observation of natural forms and flora, are similarly found in the carvings of the Pacific people. They form a universal language, a link to other distant cultures.

Ann Robinson, printed statement, supplied in 2002

Square Nikau

Lost-wax cast
Auckland, New Zealand, 2001
Height 51cm
Gift of Jennifer Robinson
V&A: C.7-2002
Exhibited, *Ann Robinson*, Galerie Jean-Paul Chapelotte, Luxembourg, 2001

Training
1965–68, 1980 Diploma of Fine Arts, Elam School of Fine Arts (sculpture, bronze-casting, glass-casting) Auckland University, New Zealand

Professional/international
1980–89 Partner in Sunbeam Glassworks (glass-blowing studio, with John Croucher and Garry Nash)

1993, 1995 Elliott Brown Gallery, Seattle

2001 Jean-Paul Chapelotte Gallery, Luxembourg

Teaching
1990–92 Part-time teaching, Carrington Polytechnic, (now UNITEC) Auckland

1991, 1996, 2000 Pilchuck Glass School, Washington State

Bruno Romanelli

1968 Born Fulford, North Yorkshire, England

Artist's statement

Boxed is one in a series of pieces which represents a period of time when my work became involved with notions of identity. Continuing themes of memory and masculinity are also present.

The boxed torso represents the way, as human beings, we are compelled to label and categorize everything, including ourselves and each other. We tend to identify each other and ourselves by the various 'boxes' into which we compartmentalize the different aspects of our lives.

BR, 2003

Boxed 3
Lost-wax cast
London, 1999
Height 48.3cm
Gift of Adrian Sassoon Esq
V&A: C.58-1999
Exhibited, Contemporary Applied Arts,
London, 1999

Training
1987–88 York College of Art & Technology, foundation course, Art and Design

1988–91 North Staffordshire Polytechnic, BA (Hons) Glass design

1993–95 Royal College of Art, MA Glass & Ceramics

Professional/international
1991–93 Assistant to Colin Reid (q.v.); Galerie L, Hamburg

1996, 1998, 2003 Clara Scremini Gallery, Paris

Teaching
1996–97 Visiting lecturer, University of Sunderland

1998 Visiting lecturer, Staffordshire University

Other works in the V&A's collection
Ex-collection: V&A Glass Gallery entrance sign letter, 'S', cast glass

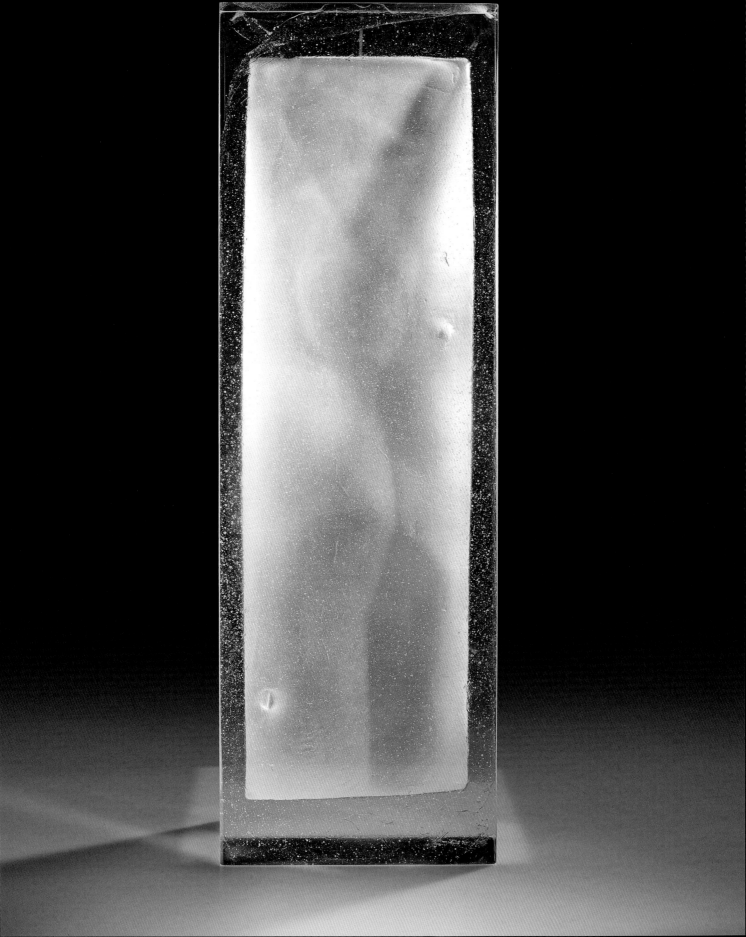

Markku Salo

1954 Born Nokia, Finland

Critical comment

Although made at the commercial glassworks, Iittala, at Nuutajärvi, Finland, this is a unique artwork. Salo makes no further claims for the title which is taken from Milan Kundera's book, *The Unbearable Lightness of Being*. 'It seemed to suit,' he says. The large bag-like form has an unexpected tension and its bulging, air-filled, pregnant presence is juxtaposed uncomfortably with the just-balanced filigree lid. It is difficult to lift and hold; it is light yet unnervingly ungraspable. All of Salo's work has an uneasy challenging edge to it; far from being merely interesting or quirky a definite sense of prickliness and discomfort effectively demolishes any easy assumptions. The body has been blown into a loosely-shaped mould made of metal mesh; the lid is made of coloured canes of glass fused together, blown and spun into a disk.

JHO, unpublished, for the exhibition *New Finnish Glass*, V&A, 1997

Unbearable Lightness

Mould-blown and filigree
Nuutajärvi glassworks, iittala oy ab, Finland, 1994
Height 45.6cm
Gift of the Artist
V&A: C.194:1,2-1997
Exhibited, *Finnish Postwar Glass*, Vardy Gallery, University of Sunderland 1996, *New Finnish Glass*, V&A, 1997
Illustrated, Jack Dawson, *Finnish Postwar Glass*, University of Sunderland, 1996, pl.53

Training

1972–74 Kankaanpää Art School

1974–79 University of Industrial Arts, Helsinki

Professional/international

1978–83 Designer, SLO group (light fittings); Destern Oy (industrial design); Ergonomia Design; Salora Oy, electronic product design

1983–91 Full-time designer, Hackman Oy Ab Nuutajärvi glassworks

1989 Galerie Inart, Amsterdam

1990 Georg Jensen Prize, Denmark

1992 Oslo Museum of Applied Arts, Norway; freelance designer, Hackman Designor Oy Ab

1995 Galerie beim Roten Turm, Germany

1995 Galerie Birgitte Kurzendörfer, Pilsach, Germany

1996, 1998 *Venezia Aperto Vetro*, invited artist

1997 Gallery Mokkumto, Seoul

2000 Gallery Blås & Knada, Stockholm

2001 Galleria De Crescenzo e Viesti, Rome

Teaching

1982–83, 1991, 1996–99 University of Industrial Arts, Helsinki

Other works in the V&A's collection

V&A: C.12&A-1998 *Rubini*; V&A: C.13&A-1988 *Farokin Majakka* (*Farok's lighthouse*); V&A: C.181-1997 *Yellow Head*, from the series, *Animals;* V&A: C.189:1,2-1997 *Chariot*, from the series, *Journey to Troy*; and glass designed for Iittala-Nuutajärvi production

Laura Diaz de Santillana

1955 Born Venice, Italy

Critical comment

The new pieces, like every single other thing that de Santillana has produced throughout her lengthy career, are elegant above all else. The compressed shapes have been likened to books, tablets and envelopes, as well as to pillars and prehistoric standing stones. De Santillana views them as bricks. She states that her thoughts are never far from architecture and, with every design, 'I am doing a little construction'. The simple architectural blocks belie the tension of the process and only the trained observer will appreciate the complexity and finesse of Simone Cenedese's fabrication. Despite its monumentality, the new series feels light. The large *Titans* appear white, but they are blown from achingly transparent gray glass encased in a layer of colourless…

Susanne K Frantz, from Barry Friedman Ltd, *Laura de Santillana: Titan*, New York, 2002, p.10

Artist's statement

It is a piece made of two cups of clear glass joined together (*incalmo* technique). Before joining the two cups we put some 'smoke' on the rim of the cups (iridescence), and then the bubble thus formed was covered with clear glass again (*sommerso* technique). Finally a silver leaf was applied on the mouth of the piece to 'seal' it.

L DdeS, 2003

Opposites and Complementaries

(light and dark, translucency/opacity)
Here the choice was that of working on completely clear pieces, and on very dark ones, almost impenetrable to light. The clear pieces would live only through light, each variation in the perception would happen because of the light embodied in the glass. The dark ones, instead, would make visible the surface and the liquidity of the material, where one could see the original form of glass, when you work on it as a molten mass, and the way this process leaves traces in the final pieces, (imprinting) In these dark pieces, light reflects instead of transpiercing the piece and the effect is inverse of the clear pieces.

Size and Proportions

Size and proportions have often been my only starting points, as I have been working with a form that can be in some ways assimilated to a canvas.

L DdeS, 'Ragas (working notes)' in Attilia Dorigato (introduction), *Laura de Santillana Works*, Silvana Editoriale, Milan, 2001

Untitled

Blown glass (*incalmo* and *sommerso* techniques) with applied silver leaf
Venice, 2002
Height 31.2 cm
Anonymous Gift
V&A: C.157-2003
The glass blown by Simone Cenedese at Cenedese glassworks, Venice, under the artist's supervision. Although untitled, this work is a forerunner of the *Titan* series.

Training

1972 Self-taught flameworking

1975–76 School of Visual Arts, New York (Graphics and Design)

Professional/international

1975–77 Graphic designer, Vignelli Associates, New York

1975–85 Art director, Venini, Venice

1985 Coburg Glass Prize for outstanding achievement, Germany; designer, then art director of Eos, glass company

1996 Contemporary Art Centre, Utrecht, The Netherlands; designing for Rosenthal

1996, 1997, 1999, 2001 Sanske Galerie, Zürich, Switzerland

1996, 1998 *Venezia Aperto Vetro*, invited artist

1997, 1999, 2001 Elliott-Brown Gallery, Seattle

1998 Gallery Tryangle, Tokyo; Daphne Johns Contemporary Art, London; Galerie l'Arc en Seine, Paris

2001 David Lusk Gallery, Memphis, Tennessee; Giorgio Armani, New York

2002 Barry Friedman Gallery, New York

Teaching

1996–98 Pilchuck Glass School, Washington State

Naoko Sato

1964 Born Nagano, Japan

Critical comment

Naoko Sato is interested in the human body. She describes this in its absence, yet its presence is intensely palpable in her glass. Conjuring glass into fabric, its fall describes the sweep of an arm or twist of a torso. Self-contained forms, as regularly pleated as a Fortuny or Issey Miyake dress, swoop and swirl, lingeringly describing a just-departed woman – like a cloud of perfume. Until recently she has kept within a smoothly elegant mode but this example, the first of its type, leads directly on to her latest glass. Less than elegant, it has a more uncomfortable dynamism; the glass is less finished than before. Since this work she has been content to keep that rawness and even to celebrate it with black and grey eruptions in the glass surface. Sato's glass is made in a modified version of lost-wax bronze casting. The resulting glass, in the form of a pleated tube, is then reheated until it softens and falls to a distance determined by the artist. The grey eruptions, accidental but welcome, are small specks of wax caught in the molten glass.

JHO, unpublished, for the exhibition *Beyond the Glass Gallery*, V&A, 2002

Artist's statement

Inspirations

I have always been interested in the way clothes find their shape on the human body. I love watching a woman with a pleated skirt walking by, creating a wonderful movement. I tried to express this interest in the medium of glass by casting, then stretching the cast piece in the kiln a second time. I hope I have managed to capture the elegant movement of textiles in my glass pieces.

NS, 2001

Transition 27
Lost-wax cast and slumped glass
London, 2001
Length 42.5cm
Gift of Adrian Sassoon Esq
V&A: C.105-2001
Exhibited, *Beyond the Glass Gallery*, V&A, 2002

Training
1993–94 Central St Martin's School of Art, foundation course

1994–96 Middlesex University, BA (Hons), (Glass Design)

1997–99 Royal College of Art, London, MA (Glass)

Professional/international
2000–present Independent artist

2002 Artist-in-residence, Alastair Pilkington Studio, North Lands Creative Glass, Lybster, Scotland; Clara Scremini Gallery, Paris

Per B Sundberg

1964 Born Stockholm, Sweden

Artist's statement

Ceramics and glass are the two materials I have been working with mostly, often in a very physical manner, bend, sting, knead, drip freely and roll in colour, sometimes I throw colour on it. But [there is] no rule without exception. It is important to explore. I do not like to be fixed with [tied to] one expression, it is anyhow a person behind it. I like functional shapes, objects to be used. Pictures and different materials and textures inspire me, new and old. I am exploring the limits of glass and want the viewer to feel something and get involved.

PBS, 2003

Fabula: Animal Faces (Djurfejs)
Hand-blown and tooled, enclosing transfers
Orrefors, 2000
Height 20.5cm
Gift of Paul Bedford
V&A: C.8-2003
Photo: Ralf Lind

Training
1983–85 Cappellagården Art School, Öland, Ceramics

1985–90 National College of Arts, Crafts & Design (Konstfack), Stockholm (under Professors Signe Persson-Melin and Oiva Toikka)

1988 Pilchuck Glass School, Washington State

1991–92 National College of Arts, Crafts & Design, Stockholm (special studentship)

Professional/international
1994–present Designer and artist, Orrefors Kosta Boda AB, Orrefors

Teaching
1993 Ceramics instructor, National College of Arts, Crafts & Design, Stockholm

1999 Ceramics instructor, Capellagården, Öland

Other works in the V&A's collection
V&A: C.9-2003 from *Fabula* series, *Guts (Tarmvred)*

Elizabeth Swinburne

1957 Born Glasgow, Scotland

Critical comment

Circles are important to Elizabeth Swinburne. The pieces in the Amsterdam show use circular forms as a recurrent motif. Large cast rings of glass, some partly encased by rough wooden casings are sombre expressions of weight and solidity...'My work was vital in channelling what I was going through and feeling. There were lots of things I wanted to say and the glass was one way of saying them. On one level it's just the feeling of the pieces, but on another it's the notion of life going in cycles. Sometimes they complete, they finish. But they always lead on – they have an effect – on another cycle. There is always a positive outcome. The pieces are not intended to be didactic statements, but looked on as a whole, bringing together the feelings and reflections following a very particular experience.'

Mike Press, 'Elizabeth Swinburne: Full Circle', *Neues Glas/New Glass*, 4/1992, pp.36–45

Artist's statement

The human touch is very important. Each of the works in the show is marked in some way by the hand. The visible presence of touch, either as an impression or as definite form. The fact that each body of work uses my hand in some way is a reflection of the concept and its multiple dimensions; the hand exists as a signature to the work.

ES, Interviewed by Shital Pattani, *Lightworks*, National Glass Centre, Sunderland, 2000, p.18

Life Cycles

Sand-cast with metal foil inclusions
Stoke-on-Trent, England, 1991
Diameter 46cm
V&A: C.8-1994
Exhibited, *Glass UK: British Contemporary Glass*, National Glass Centre, Sunderland, 1998

Training

1976–77 Brighton Polytechnic, foundation course, Art & Design

1977–81 Middlesex Polytechnic, BA (Hons) 3-D Design, Ceramics & Glass

1981–83 Gerrit Rietveld Academy, MA, under Richard Meitner (q.v.) and Mieke Groot (q.v.) Amsterdam, The Netherlands

Professional/international

1982, 1985 Galerie Arti-Choque, Velp, The Netherlands

1983 Galerie L, Hamburg, Germany; Galerie Polder, Borne, The Netherlands

1984 Galerie Nanky De Vreeze, Amsterdam, The Netherlands

1993 Galerie Ingrid Mensendiek, Düsseldorf, Germany; *The Glass Show*, London

1997 Honourable mention, Jutta Cuny-Franz Foundation, Vienna

2002 Glasmuseet Ebeltoft, Ebeltoft, Denmark

Teaching

1986–96 Head of Glass Design, Staffordshire University

1996–97 Senior lecturer, Glass department, University of Wolverhampton

1997–2000 Senior tutor in Glass, Royal College of Art, London

1999–2003 Artistic director, North Lands Creative Glass Centre, Lybster, Scotland

2000–2003 Co-ordinator in Glass, Gerrit Rietveld Academy, Amsterdam

Lino Tagliapietra

1934 Born Murano, Italy

Critical comment

'When I was young I loved Henry Moore. Everyone saw his work at the Biennale in Venice and then all of Murano loved Henry Moore…The transmission of "big art" into my work was very important. It increases your vocabulary to see what is going on there.' The sculptor Henry Moore …was noted precisely for the approach to the object that Lino espouses: Moore's work, when seen from different angles, can dissolve or coalesce. Rather than sculpting an object in the round, Moore forces the viewer to take a point of view…Although much of Lino's work does not rely on the relationship between transparent foreground and background layers, it is, for example, the core element of the *Bilbao* series. Lino's inspiration for the series came from 'geometrical contrasts' he saw in photographs of Frank Gehry's Guggenheim Museum in Bilbao. The multiplicity of Gehry's shells inspired Lino to use numerous *incalmos* (separate bubbles of glass that are joined together). Some of Lino's *Bilbaos* have ten or even more *incalmos*. Moreover, Lino often varies each layer in color and the rhythm of the canes. Lino's *Bilbaos* tend to have a great deal of clear glass in them so that the viewer's gaze can penetrate the piece, visually combining the near and far sides from any given point of view. But, like Gehry's building, Lino creates a main entrance. He explains, 'I put a lens on one side of the piece to give an idea of a point of view of a complex thing.' The lens, however, is usually placed off-center so that it never quite acts like the singular point from which the asymmetrical object must be viewed. Instead it gives an entrance – a clear starting point into what could otherwise seem like a visual labyrinth.

Daniel Kany, *La Ballata del Vetro Soffiato*, William Traver Gallery, Seattle, 2002, p.12

When I saw Lino that was a big deal. Not to make a huge deal out of one moment, but that was a big deal. After that, every time Lino came to Seattle, I was present and my technical abilities changed dramatically each time I was exposed to him. Lino is the master, and that says it all. His command of the glassmaking language is unmatched.

Dante Marioni, from Tina Oldknow, *Dante Marioni Blown Glass*, Hudson Hills Press, New York, 2000, p.25

Artist's statement

I work in three dimensions to make two-dimensional effects. This is what I mean when I say my work is often a graphic discourse. It is dynamic. It is like an image that keeps changing rather than a sculpture that you might simply see from different sides. This is an important part of my work, and I say it is like research for me because these things are so elusive.

LT, from *La Ballata del Vetro Soffiato*, William Traver Gallery, Seattle, 2002

Bilbao (from the series)
Hand-blown and wheel-cut (*battuto*)
Seattle, 2001
Height 79cm
Gift of the artist
V&A: C.1-2004
Wheel-cutting by Eamonn O'Hara under the artist's direction

Training
1945 Apprenticeship with Archimede Seguso, Murano

Professional/international
1955–65 Vetreria Galliano Ferro, Murano

1956 Achieves status of *maestro*

1966–67 Venini & Co, Murano

1968–76 Founded, and chief *maestro* at La Murrina, Murano

1977–89 Chief *maestro* and art director, Effetre International

1981 First works with AD Copier and Dale Chihuly (q.v.)

1988 Museum Boymans-van Beuningen, Rotterdam, The Netherlands

1989 Clara Scremini Gallery, Paris

1989–present Independent artist

1993 Osiris Gallery, Brussels; La Difference Galerie, Paris

1994 Nakama Gallery, Japan

1996 Rakow Commission award, Corning Museum of Glass, New York State

1996, 1998 *Venezia Aperto Vetro*, guest of honour, invited guest

1997 Glass Art Society lifetime achievement award

Teaching
1976, 1978, 1981 Workshops at La Scuola Internazionale del Vetro, Murano

1979–present Innumerable teaching at many centres internationally

Other works in the V&A's collection
V&A: C.7-1993 Bowl (for Effetre), *Rainbow*

Yoshihiko Takahashi

1958 Born Tokyo, Japan

Critical comment

Takahashi is constantly on the move, always looking for new ways to engage with glass and to explore his own creativity. Only a year before this work was made, in *The Glass Skin* (p.104) Yoriko Mizuta said:

'Lately he has been exploring the ultimate questions for an artist. Why does the artist create? What is the meaning of intentional creation? His pursuit of an essential way of creating glass art reflects his efforts to answer these questions…By presenting extraordinary circumstances in a scale beyond our daily sense of measurement, the works of Yoshihiko Takahashi emphasize how things can take on a very different appearance.'

The sculptures Takahashi showed in 1997 at that ground-breaking exhibition were of blown glass, enamelled, sand-blasted or abraded, with elements of optical glass rods, the composition a moveable assemblage yet apparently carefully considered, the scale an impressive three metres or more. One year later, he has abandoned the emphasis on cold-working and instead has returned to an earlier interest in hot glass, opting for a direct engagement with the molten material. This present work, *Holes*, is pure Abstract Expressionism. He has said that he begins with no clear plan in mind – that the glass itself suggests decisions along the way. In this sculpture, although it is relatively modest in size, he has achieved monumentality not just through the obviously weighty quantity of material but also through its sheer physicality. The action of dropping the pierced upright form headlong into the receiving cushion of hot glass is forever arrested in time, at the optimum moment.

JHO, 2004

Holes (Ana)

Gathered, poured, tooled and manipulated
Tsukui, Kanagawa, 1998
Height 43cm
V&A: FE.13-2004
Exhibited, *50 Maîtres: les arts appliqués dans le Japon contemporain*, Espace des Arts Mitsukoshi, Etoile, Paris, 1999
Photo: Taku Saiki

Training

Tama University of Art, 3-D Design Department, Product Design, Craft Design Course, Tokyo

Professional/international

1984, 1986 Glas Galerie Nordend, Munich, Germany

1985 Established Takahashi Glass Studio, Tsuki, Japan, Kanagawa Prefecture

1991 Artist-in-residence, Canberra School of Art, Australia; *The Glass Skin*, Japan

1999 Chappel Gallery, Boston

Teaching

Teaching assistant, 3-D Design Department, Tama Art University

1982–84 Glashaus am Wasserturm, Rheinbach, Germany

1991 Lecturer, Toyama City Institute of Glass Art, Toyama, Japan; guest lecturer, School of Art & Design, Sydney, Tama Art University and Tokyo Institute of Glass Art

1994 Artist-in-residence, Kanazawa Udatsuyama Crafts Workshop Centre, Kanazawa

1995–present Part-time faculty: Tama Art University, Tokyo Kokusai Glass Institute; Kanazawa Udatsuyama Craft Centre

1996 Lecturer, Aichi University of Art

1997 Omura Glass Workshop, Narita

1999 Instructor, Pilchuck Glass School, USA

Emma Woffenden

1962 Born Watford, England

Critical comment

'In a mould blown piece the glass is under incredible compression, as if it has a skin outside and liquid inside. You see the power behind the blowing and the feeling of fullness and inflation, which is very important to me. The feeling of sealed, compressed air, of contraction and expansion is exciting. There is a kind of tension.' Works such as *Pulse* and *Breath* exemplify these thoughts, in which expansion and contraction of the body's actions parallel feelings about the self in the world and about relationships. *Pulse* is relaxed, passive, while the bell jar form in *Breath*, entrapping like a lung, induces a paradoxical sense of active panic and measured calm. There is an allusion to medical and chemical apparatus and conditions, but also about a correspondence to poetic expression, such as Sylvia Plath's novel *The Bell Jar* and Marina Abramowicz's performance work in which Abramowicz and her lover seal their mouths together for 17 minutes so that the act of breathing, literally and metaphorically, tests their commitment.

Martina Margetts, 'Emma Woffenden', *Glass Magazine*, Spring, 1996, p.38

Emma Woffenden describes the transparency of glass as 'evocative of an amniotic bag'. She repeatedly returns to the bubble shape of the foetus, egg and sperm, not only as a formal language, but as expressions of touch or gesture.

Susanne K Frantz, *The Other Side of the Looking Glass; the Glass Body and Its Metaphors*, Turtle Bay Exploration Co, California, 2002, p.44

Breath

Mould-blown, cut and drilled
London, 1994
Height 25.5cm
Gift of Alastair Pilkington Fund
V&A: C.20-1995
Exhibited, *New Maker*, Contemporary Applied Arts Gallery, 1995

Training
1981–84 West Surrey College of Art & Design, BA (Hons) 3-D Design, Glass

1983 Exchange program, Tyler School of Art, Philadelphia

1991–93 Royal College of Art, MA, Ceramics & Glass, London

Professional/international
1989–91 The Glass Studio, gallery and studio joint enterprise with Jacqueline Allwood (engraving), Caroline Swash (stained glass) and Angela Thwaites (cast glass)

1994–present Own studio, London

1997–99 'Transglass' label, a design and production collaboration with Tord Boontje

Teaching
2003 External examiner, Gerrit Rietveld Academy, Amsterdam

Rachael Woodman

1957 Born Watford, UK

Critical comment

Rachael Woodman's intense free-blown colour on sweepingly vertical forms…her sensitively spaced groups of bottles, tapering slightly towards the top and slightly leaning…explored the air cleanly and with confidence.

David Whiting, 'A Celebration of Glass'; *Crafts*, no. 155, November/December, 1998, reviews, p.54

In her latest work Rachael Woodman achieves a…pitch of emotional intensity, although her expression is lateral rather than literal, abstract rather than representational, and the driving force is her Christian faith…Varying degrees of transparency, translucency and opacity – subtle qualities which only glass can embody – evoke the mysterious, tantalizing tangibility and intangibility of spiritual faith. 'The vocabulary is familiar,' says Woodman, 'but I feel that with these pieces I have something worth saying.'

Lesley Jackson, *Rachael Woodman*, Contemporary Applied Arts Gallery, London, 2001

Artist's statement

Empty Vessels, the title of this piece, is a double word play. On the one hand, it makes reference to the *Watchmen* series of previous years, pieces composed of a white inner core and a transparent outer tube. On the other hand, *Empty Vessels* is a comment on the fact that, although notionally vessel-forms, these elements are in fact part of a colour composition, a three-dimensional painting, that could only be realized in glass.

RW, statement provided for the work's display at SOFA, Chicago, 2002

Empty Vessels

Hand-blown
Frome, Somerset, 2002
Height 71.5cm
Gift of Adrian Sassoon Esq
V&A: C.125:1-11-2003
Hand-blown by Neil Wilkin under the artist's direction
Exhibited, SOFA, Chicago, 2002

Training

1975–76 Bristol Polytechnic, Art & Design, foundation course

1976–79 North Staffordshire Polytechnic, BA (Hons) Glass, Stoke-on-Trent

1980 Orrefors Glass School, Sweden

1982–84 Royal College of Art, London, MA, Glass

Professional/international

1984–87 Wilkin & Woodman Glass, with Neil Wilkin (q.v.), Bath

1985–2003 Designer, Dartington Crystal

1988 S. Wassibauer Gallery, *Kunstformen Jetzt!*, Salzburg, Austria; Galerie L, Hamburg, Germany

1991 Corning Glass Prize

1993 *The Glass Show*, London

2000 Glas Galerie Leerdam, The Netherlands

2003 Freelance design for Wedgwood glass

2003–present Freelance design for Norceram

Other works in the V&A's collection

V&A: C.240-1986 bowl
V&A: C.225-1991 dish, *Graal*
V&A: C.232-1993 vase
V&A: C.67:1-10-1997 *Canoes*
V&A: C.91-1997 *Bevelled Bowl*
And glass designed for Dartington Crystal production

Koichiro Yamamoto

1969 Born Nagoya, Japan

Critical comment

Koichiro Yamamoto claims as one of his most formative influence the displays in the V&A. 'There were a lot of vessels and pots but they were always in the show cabinets. You couldn't touch them. You couldn't use them. You used to be able to, they used to have a function, but now they are just sitting there.' Yamamoto's inclusion in this display brings his glass full circle. He trained as a designer, and in making this *Jug and Mug* he not only thoroughly negates the concept of function – normally the designer's primary concern - but he also comments on the Museum's vessels' loss of usefulness. Instead they – and his glass – have acquired a new function, that of visual appeal. Even odder, the missing handle is more clearly visible by its absence than the solid vessel within which it has been subsumed. These works are cast in moulds in which the handle-shapes, in the form of tubes connected to the outside, project into the interior.

JHO, unpublished text for *Beyond the Glass Gallery*, V&A, 2002

Artist's statement

'I am an artist not a designer,'…His origins as a designer are in mass-produced glassware but his urge is that of a sculptor…

From an unattributed, undated photocopy, provided by the Crafts Council, on file

My work originates from the idea that vessels in museums do not fulfil their original function, which is to store water, or to be filled with food. Their physical function has been transformed into a visual function, some-thing to be seen. The same things have happened in craft. Take a vase, for example, people do not always use a vase for its real purpose. They appreciate it as an object. There are unlimited key words I could use to describe my work: concrete, abstract, visual perception, intimacy and instantaneous. In terms of function, the elements which suggest function produce the object that rejects function. This reflects an irony towards the society which has regarded functionalism or efficiency as important.

KY, *ConGRADUATED*, exhibition catalogue, Glasmuseum, Ebeltoft, Denmark, 1999, p.16

Jug and Mug 6
Cast glass
London, 2001
Height of jug: 21.2cm
Gift of Paul Bedford
V&A: C.106:1,2-2001

Training
1987–92 University of Tsukuba
(BA, Industrial Design)

1996–98 Royal College of Art, London
(MA, Glass)

Professional/international
1992–96 Tokyo Glass Company, Japan

1999–2000 Artist-in-residence, Drumcroon,
Wigan, England

2001 Clara Scremini Gallery, Paris

Teaching
2000 Part-time lecturer, University of Central
Lancashire

2001 Part-time lecturer, Surrey Institute of
Arts and Design

Dana Záměčníková

1945 Born Prague, Czechoslovakia (now Czech Republic)

Critical comment

When they are small, Záměčníková's condensed images are detailed and,
literally, controlled. While these images maybe surreal, their miniaturized
world is not threatening. Everybody likes them. However, everybody does
not like the life-sized ones. When her images are enlarged, the artist
becomes the aggressor and her sculpture becomes a body blocking our
path – a body that, in its brittleness, is a potential weapon. These images
are confrontational: a barking dog, an accusing stare, a creature that is
half-human and half-animal. The drawing style changes; it becomes
sketchy and graffiti-like, sometimes splashed with paint. In the past, light
passing through glass symbolized divine purity. Záměčníková scrubs and
scratches it making it 'slightly dirty', slightly human. In her words she
'goes against the glass', muddying it and forcing the viewer to imagine
more of the story than is provided.

**Susanne K Frantz, *The Glass Skin*, Corning Museum of Glass/Kunstmuseum
Düsseldorf/Hokkaido Museum of Modern Art, 1998, p.122**

Artist's statement

Thanks to the architecture and stage-design which I have been studying, it
seems to me that space is almost a matter of course. It means not to
perceive things torn out of space but, on the contrary, always to try to see
and to understand these things within a wider context. I try to render and
to express chains of events in both spatial and semantic relationships. I
look for things which belong to each other, to the family, to history, as well
as to the present, i.e., which belong to human space and time.

**DZ, from *Form, Light, Glass: Contemporary Glass from the Czech Republic*,
American Craft Museum, NYC, 1996**

Divided World (formerly known as
Old Woman)
Sheet glass, painted in enamel colours
Prague, 1990
Length 187cm
V&A: C.117-1992
Illustrated as *Divided World*, in *Dana
Záměčníková*, privately published, Czech
Republic, no date

Training
1962–68 Czech Technical University, School
of Architecture, Prague

1969–72 Academy of Applied Arts, Prague,
under Professor Josef Svoboda

Professional/international
1984, 1986, 1987, 1991, 1995, 2000 Heller
Gallery, New York

1985 Galerie Gottschalk-Betz,
Frankfurt-am-Main

1986 Galerie L, Hamburg

1990 Clara Scremini Gallery, Paris

1992 Kanazawa, Grand Prize, Japan;
commisioned artwork, *Glasswall*, The World
Bank, Washington DC

1993 Commisioned artwork, sculpture,
Corning, New York

1996 Maurine Littleton Gallery, Washington,
DC; *Venezia Aperto Vetro*, invited artist

1998–99 *The Glass Skin*, Japan

Teaching
1983, 1986, 1989, 1996 Instructor and
artist-in-residence, Pilchuck Glass School,
Washington State

1986–2003 Various lectures, workshops,
artist-in-residences etc in USA, England,
Australia, Mexico, Japan, New Zealand,
Portugal, Korea and Ireland

Other works in the V&A's collection
V&A: C.98-1986 *Two Cats*

Toots Zynsky

1951 Born Boston, Massachusetts, USA

Critical comment

'It's really like painting,' [she] says. 'It's an identical thought-process – the way you build up a painting or drawing then the other layers go on really to hold together so it's actually about thirty layers of thread. They are very solid, they look more fragile than they are.' She works in glass, but her inspiration comes from elsewhere, and she cites birds and the sea in particular. Her forms set colours in motion, creating an almost kinetic effect. The threads of which the vessels are composed give the glass the vibrant quality of taut wire. The effect is one of arrested movement …When it comes to colour…she understands better than anybody how to use the luminosity of colour. Hers is a very personal colour idiom, without the transparent qualities normally associated with glass. Zynsky's colours do not absorb light, they bounce it back at you. She creates the illusion of having applied colours with brushstrokes. She uses colours to stir the senses…

Dan Klein, *Artists in Glass*, Mitchell Beazley, London, 2001, pp.228–229

Dondolante Serena 2000

Drawn glass thread, fused, slumped, and hot-worked (*filet-de-verre* technique)
Providence, RI, 2000
Length 61cm
Gift of Dale and Doug Anderson through the American Friends of the V&A
V&A: C.141-2003

Training

1970 Haystack Mountain School of Crafts, Deer Isle, Maine

1971 Pilchuck Glass School, Washington State

1971–73 Rhode Island School of Design, B.F.A., Providence

1979 Rhode Island School of Design, advanced glass program

Professional/international

1981–82 Founding member of second New York Experimental Glass Workshop (now UrbanGlass)

1981–83 Freelance designer for Venini & Co, limited editions, Murano, Italy

1984 Artist-in-residence, UCLA, Los Angeles, California

1984–85 Ghana, special music research project

1988 Rakow Commission, Corning Museum of Glass, New York State

1991–92 Freelance designing and executing limited edition pieces for Eos, Murano, Italy

2001–02 Ebeltoft Glass museum, Denmark and Museo Correr, Venice

Teaching

1979–present Freelance instructor and lecturer to many courses and conferences in USA, England, Japan, Switzerland, France and Mexico

1981–2 Department head of Hot Glass Program, New York Experimental Glass Workshop

1984 Instructor, Pilchuck Glass School, Washington State

1986–87 External examiner, West Surrey College of Art, Farnham, England

The following is a list of glass artists in the V&A, other than those in the main illustrated section of this book. For reasons of space, this list shows only those whose work between 1980 and 2004 is in the Collection. For glass artists before 1980, and all stained and painted glass panels, please contact the Museum.

Maria Ajike Amidu (UK) C.44-1996 *Trace Elements Two*

Monica Backström (Swed) C.107-1988 *Egg*; C.108&A-C-1988 *Astronaut's Thermos*

Jane Beebe (UK) C.226-1991 bowl, Dartington limited edition; designs for production

Gru Bergslien (Nor) C.157-1988 vase; designs for Hadeland production

Brian Blanthorn & Jenny Blanthorn (UK) C.241-1986; C.67-1994 dishes

Sandy Bowden (UK) C.95-1982 bowl

Michael Boylen (USA) Circ.277-1972 untitled

Ulla Mari Brantenberg (Nor) C.149&A&B-1988 *Three Independent Lives*

Amanda Brisbane (UK) C.57-1990 *Crocodile*

Keith Brocklehurst (UK) C.35-1992 *Whisper Bowl*

Jane Bruce (UK) C.121-1979 bowl; C.8-2004 *Sentinel*

Thomas Buechner III (USA) C.170-1986 *Lavender Spun Piece*

Dillon Clarke (UK) C.134-137-1979 vases and bowl

Ros Conway (UK) C.69-1998 *Nereid III*

Gunnar Cyrén (Swed) C.81-1994 *Dalby*; and designs for Orrefors production

Tatiana Best Devereux (UK) C.205&A-1984 untitled

Peter Dreiser (UK) C.179-1977 (goblet); C.108-1980 paperweight

Ben Edols & Kathy Elliott (Austral) C.7-2004 *Leaf*

Eva Englund (Swed) C.181-1986 *The Sea Maid*; designs for Orrefors production

Ulla Forsell (Swed) C.35&A-1989 *Secret Box*

Peter Furlonger (UK) C.110-1994 *Tree of Life*

Michael Glancy (USA) C.56-1981 untitled

Hilary Green (UK) C.227-1991 vase, Dartington limited edition; designs for production

Peter Hanauer (UK) C.92&A&B-1982 jugs

Elaine Harré (UK) C.175-1981 goblet

William Heesen (Neth) Circ.244-1960 plaque; C.119-1984 bottle

Lars Hellsten (Swed) C.192-1986 *Shell*

Sam Herman (UK/USA) Circ.765-1967 bottle; Circ.646-1969 untitled; Circ.387-1971 bowl; Circ.213-1971 bottle; Circ.214-1971 untitled; Circ.215-1971 *3 Vertical Forms*; C.27-1980 bottle; C.107-1981 *Deep, Round, Red Form*

Darryle Hinz (USA/Den) C.93-1982 plate

Ulrica Hydman-Vallien (Swed) Circ.455-1974 *Tintomara*; C.179-1986 *Snakes in Love*; C.106-1988 *Lovelady*

David Kaplan & Annica Sandström (UK) C.223-1987 bowl

Karen Klim (Nor) C.159-1988 *From the Bottom of the Sea*; C.160-1988 *Snake Glass*; C.161-1988 *Briar Rose*

Erika Lagerbielke (Swed) C.69-1954 *The Lion Heart*, Orrefors limited edition; designs for production

Louis Leloup (Belg) C.5-1980 untitled; C.6-1980 vase; C.1-3-1993 vases

Michal Machat (Cz) C.38:1,2-1992 *Charlie*

Gillian Manning Cox (UK) C.286-1987 *Free*

Ivana Masitová (Cz) C.201-1991 untitled; C.202-1991 bottle

Mark Matthews (USA) C.25,26-1996 *Predator Spheres*

David Maude-Roxby-Montalto (UK) C.10-1996 goblet

Sara McDonald (UK) C.19-1991 dish

Alison McConachie (UK) C.96-1982 bowl

Carol McNicholl (UK) C.144-1993 jug, with Steven Newell

Annette Meech (UK) C.29-1978 untitled; C.9-1980 vase

Jon & Deb Meyer (USA) C.61-1981 vase

Charmian Mocatta (UK) C.111-1994 *Best Fruits Ripen Slowly*

Isgard Moje-Wohlgemuth (Ger) Circ.296-1973 beaker; C.92-1981 vase

Simon Moore (UK) C.348-1983 dish; C.209-1985 vase; C.41-1990 vase; C.200-1991 candelabra; C.39-1994 bowl; C.40:1,2 to C.42:1,2-1994 decanters; C.43:1,2,-1994 jar and cover; C.44-1994 candlestick; C.45-1994 jug

Carl Nordbruch (UK) C.104-2001 *Waiting for Something*

Thomas Patti (USA) C.57-1981 *Solar Gray Riser*

David Peace (UK) Circ.608&A&B-1962 *Sanctuary Lamp*; Circ.370-1976 tray; C.300-1993 *Life is not a cup to be drained...*

Ronald Pennell (UK) C.242-1986 *Summer Night on the River*

David Pilkington (UK) C.112-1994 *Filigree Form: Sonnets*

Stephen Procter (UK) C.16-1981 *The Expansive Thought*; C.85-*1982 Reciprocating Thought*; C.224&A-1987 *Double Gatherer*

David Prytherch (UK) C.9-1996 *Pavane*

Clifford Rainey (UK/USA) C.70-1982 *Belfast After Pollaiuolo*

René Roubícek (Cz) C.21-1998 *Kohlrabi*

Karlin Rushbrooke (UK) C.65-1994 bowl

Timo Sarpaneva (Fin) Circ.356-1965 *Eruption*; C.197-1987 *Claritas*; designs for Iittala art and production

Ivana Srámková-Solcová (Cz) C.203-1991 bottle

John Smith (UK) C.80:1,2-1995 *What! Watt's Whatnot!*

Pauline Solven (UK) C.28-1978 dish; C.102-1981 vase and tablewares for Cowdy Glass

Anthony Stern (UK) C.215-1983 vase; C.216-1983 dish

Denji Takeuchi (Jap) FE.4-1995 *Composition No.162*

David Taylor (UK) C.190&A-1980; C.36:1,2:1992 perfume bottles

Dalibor Tichý (Cz) C.96-1986 *Wings*

Oiva Toikka (Fin) Circ.444-1969 *Lollipop Isle*; Circ.462-1969 *Kurkkupurkki*; C.40-1988 *Year Cubes*; C.41&A-1988 *Snow Castle*; C.28:1,2-1994 *Sonja*; designs for Nuutajärvi glassworks production

Sybren Valkema (Neth) C.98-1982 *Mask*; C.99-1982 untitled; C.100-1982 bowl

Bertil Vallien (Swed) C.110-1988 *Destination X*; designs for Kosta Boda art lines and production

Ann Wärff (Wolff) (Swed) C.162-1984 bowl; C.163&A-1984 bowl & stand; C.17&A-1987 *The Number is Two*

Goran Wärff (Swed) C.178-1986 *Glass is Liquid*

Steven Weinberg (USA) C.82,83-1991 untitled

Neil Wilkin (UK) C.228-1991 bowl, Dartington limited edition

Christopher Williams (UK) C.69-1982 bowl; C.10-1980 bowl

Robert Willson (USA) C.226-1985 *Madonna*

Naoto Yokoyama (Jap) FE.5-1991 *Candlelight*

annealing
The process of slowly cooling a completed object in a separate part of the glass furnace or in a separate furnace. This avoids internal stresses caused by different parts of the glass cooling more quickly than others. It is an integral part of glass-making because if a hot glass object is allowed to cool too quickly, it will be highly strained by the time it reaches room temperature and may break.

battuto
Battuto (Italian: beating) is a style of **wheel-cutting**, where the surface is cut to produce innumerable small irregular markings running in the same direction.

borosilicate
Borosilicate glass, which has heat- and shock-resistant properties, was developed specifically for use in scientific laboratories by Schott in Germany, and Corning in the USA in the early years of the 20th century. When the First World War put an end to co-operation between the two, Corning went on to develop the glass as domestic ware for oven use, under the trade name Pyrex. Today it is used by some glass artists for its strength, especially in fine detail and its particular clear, yellowish tinge.

casing/cased
Glass made up of differently coloured layers. This can be made by blowing a bubble of glass inside a prepared cup of a different colour, or by dipping the first gather of molten glass in another of a different colour. The two layers fuse (perhaps with frequent reheating) and are blown until they have the desired form.

filet de verre
This term (French: glass thread) is used by Toots Zynsky to describe her own technique. She arranges drawn glass threads according to her own design. These are then fused, slumped and, on removal from the kiln while still soft, they are worked into the final shape.

flameworking
Otherwise known as lampworking: the technique by which objects are shaped from prefabricated rods and tubes of glass that, when heated in an open flame, become soft and can be manipulated into the desired shape. Today, gas-fuelled torches are used.

Graal
(Swedish: Grail) The trade name for a type of decorative glass developed at Orrefors of Sweden in 1916. The design is carved, engraved or etched on a cooled thick-walled bubble of coloured glass which is then re-heated, **cased** in a thick outer layer of transparent glass of a different colour, and blown to the required shape and size. The process of decoration may be repeated more than once between several layers.

incalmo
Incalmo (Italian: graft) technique was invented around 1600. It consists of the melting and joining of two differently coloured hemispherical 'bowls' around their rims, which are of equal diameter. A bi-coloured object is the result; the process can be repeated so that a banded object results.

kiln
An oven for heating glass at a lower temperature than that of the furnace, used to fuse enamels, and for **kiln-forming** processes such as **slumping**.

kiln-forming
Also known as kiln-casting or kiln-fusing. The process of fusing or shaping glass (usually in or over a mould) by heating it in a **kiln**.

lampworking
See under **flameworking**.

lost-wax cast
A technique adapted from metalworking. A model is made in wax, it is coated in plaster (or clay) which is then heated. The wax flows out through vents in the plaster leaving the interior clean. Molten or powdered glass is introduced into the interior via the same vents and the filled mould may be heated again. After **annealing**, the mould is removed from the glass.

pâte de verre
(French: glass paste) A material produced by grinding glass into a fine powder, adding a binder to create a paste and a fluxing medium to facilitate melting. The paste is brushed or tamped into a mould, dried, and fused by firing. After it has cooled the object is removed from the mould and finished.

reticello
Reticello filigrana was invented during the first half of the 16th century. Equal lengths of circular-sectioned clear glass rods containing white or coloured glass threads are fused and then gathered along one edge and blown to the required shape. This is called *filigrana* (Italian: filigree) glass and it comes in many forms. *Reticello* (Italian: small network) *filigrana* is made with the canes laid in a criss-cross pattern to form a fine net, which may contain tiny airtraps.

slumping
The process of shaping glass, which may already have integral decoration such as inlaid glass of different colours, by allowing it to sag through its own weight into or over a form during heating in a **kiln**.

sommerso
Thick glass that has usually been **cased** several times thus creating various colour or light effects in thick, transparent layered glass. It may include small bubbles, gold leaf etc.

Starphire
This is the trade name for the highly specialised glass used by Peter Aldridge in his sculpture.

Swedish overlay
Overlay takes the *incalmo* technique one stage further, once the rims are fused, by pulling one 'bowl' over the other. The skill is in keeping them fitted snugly, with no air trapped between. This technique was taken up especially by Swedish glassworks.

wheel-cutting, or wheel-engraving
A process of decorating the surface of glass by the grinding action of a wheel, using disks of various sizes and materials (usually copper). An abrasive grease or slurry is applied, as the engraver holds the object against the underside of the rotating wheel. For engraving, a diamond-wheel can be used.

zanfirico
See under **reticello**. *Zanfirico* is another term for filigree, and derives from the name of the Venetian antiquary, Antonio Sanquirico who in the 19th century commissioned glassworks in Murano to produce copies of historic filigree glass.

The following books provide general information on glass art

Cummings, Keith, *The Technique of Glass Forming*, BT Batsford, London, 1980 (2nd edition, 1996); *A History of Glassforming*, A&C Black, London, 2002

Dorigato, Attila, Dan Klein and Rosa Barovier Mentasti (eds), *Venezia Aperto Vetro, International New Glass*, Electa, Milan, 1996 and 1998

Frantz, Susanne K, *Contemporary Glass*, Corning Museum of Glass, 1989

Frantz, Susanne K, *The Glass Skin*, The Corning Museum of Glass/ Kunstmuseum Düsseldorf/ Hokkaido Museum of Modern Art, 1998, preface to English edition

Goodearl, Tom and Marilyn, *Engraved Glass, International Contemporary Artists*, Antique Collectors' Club, Woodbridge, 1999

Ioannou, Noris, *Australian Studio Glass, The Movement, Its Makers and Their Art*, Craftsman House, Roseville East, NSW, 1995

Klein, Dan, *Glass, a Contemporary Art*, William Collins & Co, London, 1989

Klein, Dan, *Artists in Glass, late twentieth-century masters in glass*, Mitchell Beazley, London, 2001

Layton, Peter, *Glass Art*, A&C Black, London, 1996

Oldknow, Tina, *Pilchuck: A Glass School*, Pilchuck Glass School/University of Washington Press, Seattle, 1996

Olivié, Jean-Luc and Sylva Petrova, *Bohemian Glass*, Flammarion, Paris, 1990 (English edition)

Petrova, Sylva, *Czech Glass*, Gallery, Prague, 2001

Whitehouse, David, *Glass: A Pocket Dictionary of Terms commonly used to describe glass and glassmaking*, Corning Museum of Glass, Corning, New York, 1993

The following books, exhibition catalogues and articles provide further information on the artists illustrated; see also titles in individual entries

Aldridge *New Sculpture by Peter Aldridge*, Steuben Glass, New York, 1981

Chihuly Kuspit, Donald E, *Chihuly*, Portland Press, 1997 (2nd edition, 1998)

Opie, Jennifer H (editor), *Chihuly at the V&A*, V&A, in association with Portland Press, 2001

Dejonghe *Carte Blanche à Bernard Dejonghe*, Paris, Musée des Arts Décoratifs, 1995

Fusions, Dunkirk/Dunkerque, Musée d'Art Contemporain, 1997

Dickinson Klein, Dan (introduction), *Anna Dickinson*, Galerie von Bartha, Basel, 1998

Eliáš Hoskova, Simeona (introduction), *Bohumil Eliáš*, Vydala Stredoevropská Galerie, Prague, 1994

Frijns *Bert Frijns Glas*, Haags Gemeentesmuseum, The Hague, The Netherlands, 1995

Bert Frijns: Purely Glass, Eretz Israel Museum, Tel Aviv, 1998

van Ginneke *Vincent van Ginneke*, Musée-Atelier du Verre, Sars-Poteries, 1999

Lane Opie, Jennifer H, 'Danny Lane', *Vormen uit vuur*, No.149, 1993, pp.32–39

Opie, Jennifer H, *Danny Lane's Glass, Breaking Tradition*, Mallett at Bourdon House, London, 1999, pp.10–22

Leperlier Galerie Capazza, *Antoine Leperlier 'L'Instant juste Avant'*, Paris/Nançay, 2002

Libenský Frantz, Susanne K, 'A Collaboration in Glass', *Stanislav Libenský, Jaroslava Brychtová, a 40–year collaboration in glass*, edited by Susanne K Frantz, Prestel, Munich & New York, 1994, p.37

Meitner *Richard Meitner*, Musée-Atelier du Verre, Sars-Poteries, France, 1998

Cold Fusion, Boerhaave Museum, Leiden, The Netherlands, 1996

Moje Edwards, Geoffrey, *Klaus Moje Glass, A Retrospective Exhibition*, National Gallery of Victoria, 1995

Jung-Chou, Lin and Lucinda Ward, *The Glass World of Klaus Moje*, Hsin-Chu Municipal Glass Museum, Taiwan, 2001

Morris Elliott, Kate (editor), *William Morris: Artefact and Art*, University of Washington Press, 1989

Edgar, Blake, and James Yood, *William Morris: Man Adorned*, University of Washington Press, 2001

Ohira Barry Friedman Ltd, *Yoichi Ohira: A Phenomenon in Glass*, New York, 2002

Palová Petrova, Sylva & Dan Klein, *Zora Palová – Amygdale*, University of Sunderland, 1999

Reid Museo De Arte En Vidrio De Alcorcon, *Colin Reid Glass*, Madrid, 2000

de Santillana Barry Friedman Ltd, *Laura de Santillana Titan*, New York, 2002

Vedrenne, Elisabeth, 'Laura De Santillana à l'Arc en Seine', *Laura de Santillana: Os, Or*, Paris, 2002

Tagliapietra Sarpellon, G, *Lino Tagliapietra: the Harmony of Glass*, Arsenale Editrice, Venice, 1994

Barovier, Marino (editor), *Tagliapietra, A Venetian Glass Maestro*, Vitrum: Links for Publishing, Dublin, 1998

Eliëns, Titus M, *AD Copier & Lino Tagliapietra: Inspiration in Glass*, Gemeentesmuseum den Haag, The Hague, The Netherlands, 2000

Woffenden *Emma Woffenden*, National Glass Centre, Sunderland, 1998

Zámečníková *Dana Zámečníková*, privately published, Czech Republic, no date

Many people have helped with this book. The Victoria and Albert Museum is especially grateful to those donors who have transformed the collection into one of international importance. Some deserve special mention here for their commitment to glass and to the Museum: Dale & Doug Anderson, for gifts, advice and invaluable support; for gifts of glass, Paul Bedford, Adrian Sassoon and Dan Klein. Many others are credited within the book although this hardly does justice to their great generosity; and some have chosen to remain anonymous. Many artists themselves have been especially supportive and generous in agreeing to donate to the Museum. The V&A is deeply grateful to all.

The time-consuming tasks of collecting and collating the detailed entries on so many artists are inevitably fraught with opportunities for error. I want to thank particularly Alan J Poole, of Dan Klein Associates, for patiently answering endless questions and sharing his database, and Dan Klein and Susanne K Frantz for their help. Naturally, any mistakes that have survived into print are entirely my own and I apologize for these.

In the Museum I must thank especially Terry Bloxham, for her tireless support and Sara Hodges for her careful and sympathetic photography; Reino Liefkes, especially for his help in the acquisition of Dutch and German glass; Daniel McGrath, Ian Thomas, Mike Kitcatt, Richard Davis and Christine Smith of the V&A Photographic Studio; David Wright and Rupert Faulkner, Ken Jackson, Chas McDevitt, Emma Neave, Steve Woodhouse and all my colleagues in the Ceramics & Glass Department, have each been helpful in many ways. My thanks also go to copy-editor, Colin Maitland, and designers, Broadbase. Finally, my editor, Monica Woods, has been a model of patience and efficiency.

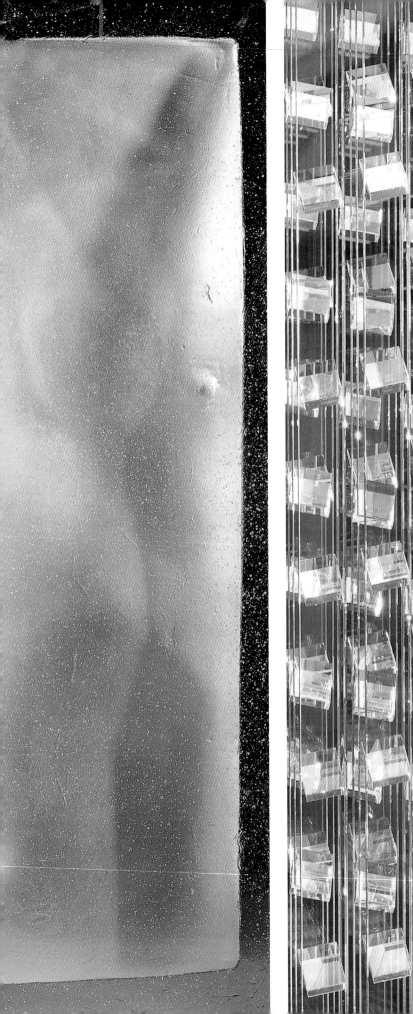